SELF-DISCIPLINE

SELF-DISCIPLINE

*Stop Procrastinating, Boost Focus and Confidence,
Control your Emotions, Build Success by Enhancing
Creativity and Productivity*

WES VIVANCO

MANERBA

Manerba books may be purchased for educational, business, or sales promotional use. For information, please email publishing@manerba.co.uk

ISBN 978-1-914459-01-6

Table of Contents

SELF-DISCIPLINE

Introduction

We live in a fast-paced world, with dynamic changes happening all around us. With billions of people on the planet, it's so easy to get carried away and lose the plot of your life. Even though at times it doesn't seem like it, everyone has a purpose on this planet. The difference is that for some, their purpose is clear, while others go about life like they are lost in an unending maze, unable to figure out what to do. This means going through life like a zombie.

Most people lose the plot because they waste a lot of time pursuing things that don't add value to their lives. Life is too precious to get through it without a sense of direction. This is the challenge that many people are going through, and unfortunately, it robs them of the joys of living a productive life.

Getting through life one day at a time, you encounter a lot of challenges like every other person. The difference is your perspective, and how you handle the challenges. Procrastination and lack of confidence, for example, are two of the biggest hindrances to progress and prosperity. You find yourself pushing an idea to the back of your mind for so long that you eventually lose the enthusiasm to pursue it, and let it go altogether. You find yourself in situations where opportunities come knocking on your door but you keep missing them because you are not bold enough.

These are simple inferences to common challenges that people go through all the time. Take a moment and think about it, have you missed an incredible opportunity recently? Is there something that you were supposed to achieve, but have been pushing aside for a long time? If you look around, you will realise that other people might be in the same situation as you are, yet somehow, they took their chances, worked on their priorities, and are forging ahead. So, what's the difference?

In this book, our concern is not on the differences, but rather, empowering you to take charge and be in control of your life. Indeed, things like procrastination and lack of confidence manifest in different ways. In some people, the effect might be subtle, while it could have significant ramifications in another person's life. The magnitude aside, this book will teach you the value of self-discipline.

To realise your purpose in life and achieve your goals, you must embrace self-discipline. While we loosely talk about self-discipline in terms of grit and motivation, there's more to it. Self-discipline is about recognizing you have a greater purpose in life and working towards it. It is about resisting immediate or instant gratification for the pursuit of wholesome, greater rewards in the future. It is about being in complete control of yourself—your thoughts, behaviour and actions.

The desire for success is commendable, but do you have the discipline to do the work, walk the talk, toe the line? This is where self-discipline comes in. Think of all the great personalities you've come across or read about. One thing that has brought them the success they boast of is self-discipline. It is realizing for what and where you are held accountable, and taking responsibility for your actions.

To succeed in your pursuits, you must embrace a life of productivity and creativity. We are talking about value addition. Look at life like wine. Why do we pay so much for a bottle of wine, but a relatively smaller sum for the grapes from which it is derived? The answer is simple, value addition. The fruits are refined through different processes, and at each stage, value is added to the process. Eventually, you end up with a bottle of wine worth hundreds of dollars, from a handful of grapes. The same concept applies in life.

Success is about value addition. Look at your social circle, for example. What value do you bring to your friends? What value do they bring to your life? Take a step back and take accountability for your actions. This is what self-discipline is about. To be successful, you will learn to identify people and things that are important to your journey, and those that you need to drop. At times you have to make tough decisions or make peace with a mediocre life.

You will learn how to boost your confidence, be bolder, and take more chances. Other than taking the opportunities that come your way, you will also learn how to identify opportunities where other people don't. All this is possible because your perspective of life changes. All this happens when you shift your focus to the bigger picture. Truly, nothing will stand in your way.

We spend so much time looking for answers to questions about our lives when the best solutions we seek lie deep within us. If you have struggled with procrastination, for example, you must make the bold decision to do something about it. Self-discipline teaches the importance of following through on your decisions, perseverance, and choosing the right choices and actions for eventual success. It will empower you to overcome procrastination, laziness, and addiction, and become confident and bold enough to push through obstacles in life.

The unfortunate reality of life is that most people know and understand the importance of self-discipline. However, very few will act on it, strengthen it, or develop it. It's like untapped resources lying deep within us, making it difficult to reach our potential.

As we discuss the different tenets of self-discipline, you will also realise that the concept is different from what most people think. Self-discipline is not about restrictions and limiting yourself. Instead, you realise that at every point in life, you always have a choice; you have decisions to make. If you make the wrong ones, you must embrace the consequences thereof, or reap the benefits if you make the right choices.

Never give up, overcome distractions, and resist temptations. You've heard these phrases more than you can remember. This is what self-discipline is about. This is how you stay the course, and achieve your goals. This is how you stay strong when everything seems to be going against you. This is how you pull yourself together after suffering a loss and bounce back stronger. This is how you build real, stable and sustainable success.

Mastering self-discipline will help you with more than overcoming procrastination and building your confidence. It helps you keep working on your goals even if you are going through a phase where you are not as enthusiastic as you were at the beginning. If you are on a diet, it will help you stay the course and commit to the end goals, avoiding the temptation of wanton cheating foods. Self-discipline can also help you create healthy routines like meditation, which is great for your overall well-being.

To develop self-discipline, you must also realise why it is important in your life. You are probably at a point where things are not going according to plan, or you need to rethink your approach to life. You should also be able to recognise denial and address undisciplined behaviour. As you increasingly become aware and conscious of undisciplined behaviour, you become more inclined to learn how to overcome and change for the better.

Everyone's crazy about the future prospects of electric vehicles. On impulse, the first name that comes to mind is Elon Musk's Tesla. What Elon Musk has achieved is enviable. Having and pursuing his purpose in life is one of the reasons why Elon Musk is one of the top business leaders of our time. His secret? Well, there are many reasons behind his success, some of which he'll probably never mention. But, a dominant theme in his speeches and interviews is self-discipline. It's no wonder he's considered a master of self-discipline.

People like Elon Musk understand that there are times in life when you will privately feel things are too hard, that you can barely go on. However, instead of calling it a day, they persist. His emphasis has always been discipline, energy, and focus. Without these three elements, you cannot succeed in life.

Make a personal commitment to emulate Elon Musk today. Take action, persist, and never give up. Find something you are truly passionate about, and give it all your attention. Self-discipline is not something you just do once, it is a decision you make daily to get up, show up, and put in the work. The fundamental part of the human brain is wired to find meaning, and the best way is by having a purpose. That is how you make a difference.

Read on, and discover how you can unlock your life's potential.

CHAPTER
ONE

Guide to Developing Self-Discipline

Quick one—how far have you come to accomplishing your New Year's resolutions? There's usually a lot of excitement around these resolutions. The promise to do and become better, to improve your life, or to achieve greater things. This is the time when many people reflect on their past and make new plans. However, a few weeks in, the excitement and enthusiasm fizzles away, and you slowly settle into your old ways. Before long, you slouch through the year, looking forward to the next time you make new resolutions, and that's if you will make them at all.

You know those moments when you slowly let go of your resolutions and decide to focus on other things? That's when self-discipline comes in handy. You see, resolutions are backed by good intentions. Most resolutions come from deep thought, reflection, and realizing the need to do better. You lay the groundwork for progress, yet you let go shortly after. Self-discipline is the only way you can stay focused on these and other goals. You learn to control your reactions to situations, and in the process, control yourself.

The thing about self-discipline and life is that you are constantly bombarded with decision-making opportunities, and for each, you must take responsibility for your choices. Everything from the time your alarm goes off, to the food you eat, to your commute to work, involves a set of choices, and to succeed in life, you must learn to make wise choices.

Self-discipline is built around persistence, hard work, and acceptance. Many people struggle in life because they live in denial. You must live in the moment and accept the reality of life, and the challenges you face. You cannot make progress while in denial about the reality of your present. Everyone starts somewhere, so your first step is to accept your ground zero, then make plans on how to improve on it.

Everyone wants to enjoy the good life, but few want to do the necessary work. Most people are inclined to do the easy stuff first, and avoid the hard stuff. Life does not come with a guarantee of an easy way out. Even those who seem to have this advantage usually work hard behind the scenes. Hard work requires concentration and determination. Note, however, that not all hard work pays off. Emphasise smart work instead. Smart work means immense planning, setting objectives, strategies, and executing your plan.

Persistence is the last piece of the puzzle. Stay true to your goals, plans, and strategy even when you lack the enthusiasm or motivation to keep going. Sports fans can relate to the emotions of a goal scored in the dying moments of the game. It's usually a bag of mixed feelings, relief, joy, and exhilaration for the winning team, but despair, disappointment, and disbelief for the conceding team. Persistence keeps you going even when odds are stacked against you, and in the long run, it pays off. The beauty of persistence is that the accumulated effort and results create a unique sense of motivation, and it pays off.

The Journey to Self-Actualization

Following these tenets of self-discipline will not just help you succeed in life, but you will also achieve a status that has proven elusive for many people—self-actualization. Self-actualization, as proposed by Abraham Maslow in his hierarchy of needs, is a psychological process where you realise your full intellectual, creative, and social potential (Maslow et al., 1998). This process is innate and varies from one person to the other. Your idea of self-actualization is not necessarily the same idea that someone else has. The common understanding of self-actualization, however, is that it takes years to accomplish.

Since self-actualization is built around pushing your limits and abilities to realise your potential, you can already see how self-discipline comes in. It is about personal growth and self-development, none of which you can achieve without self-discipline. Positive psychology is also imperative to this realization, to help you in the pursuit of enjoyment and excellence. If the processes towards reaching your potential are fulfilling, the positivity will be felt in other aspects of your life too.

Achieving self-actualization is an important goal in your journey to revitalise your life through self-discipline because of the positive impact on your well-being. Most people assume that this level of actualization is only achieved by prominent people like top business leaders. This is not true. Everyone has a different path in life, and your goals and motivation towards them will never be the same as someone else's. The push to realise your potential is a personal endeavour, and your success while at it will depend on your social, intellectual, and creative potential.

Self-actualization is not about status or money, though these are desirable statuses in society that might also give you that satisfaction. It is a state you achieve by fulfilling your potential. When you get to this point, you will realise how life is full of immense possibilities and opportunities. It is about dreaming big and achieving those dreams. It is within your reach, whether you want to become a musician, a teacher, a painter, or whatever else you are passionate about.

Self-actualization sits at the peak of Maslow's hierarchy of needs, a representation of different things that motivate our behaviour. It is a complex need, suggesting that to achieve it, all the other needs lower in the hierarchy must be achieved as well. The other needs in the hierarchy are as follows:

1. Psychological Needs

These are the most basic survival needs. In this class, we have reproduction, food and water, shelter, clothing, good health, and rest. According to Maslow, you must fulfil these needs to feel comfortable in life, and once achieved, you are psychologically prepared to achieve the next level—safety needs.

2. Safety Needs

This is about protection in every form. It could be financial security, health, well-being, protection from theft and violence, or emotional stability. Safety is a major concern in life, without which you cannot be comfortable. You will realise that life is easier as long as your safety is guaranteed. If you are in business, you go about your daily routines with confidence because you know your inventory and business, in general, are always safe. If you are in a relationship, the assurance of emotional security strengthens your trust in your partner, and you don't find yourself doubting their every move.

3. Love and Belonging Needs

These needs are about human interaction. They are fulfilled through your family and friendships. Social interactions breed different levels of emotional and physical intimacy. Such bonds give you an elevated feeling of belonging. You feel appreciated and welcome whenever you are around certain people. If these needs are not met, you can feel unwanted, like an outcast. These needs help you forge an identity within your circles, whether it's in the family, or with your colleagues at work, or the friends you hang around often. Getting these needs met delivers an elevated aspect of kinship.

4. Esteem Needs

Esteem needs—alongside self-actualization needs—are the first of the higher class of needs. These are ego-driven needs. Esteem, for example, is built around the belief that you are a valuable member and deserve dignity. Esteem is also about feeling confident in your accomplishments and potential for personal growth. Esteem needs can be realised in two ways. We have your assessment of your worth and the assessment that comes from acknowledgement and respect from people around you.

Self-actualization comes after the four needs above are met, hence the highest point in the hierarchy of needs. Things like skill development through professional courses and training, higher education, refined talents in hobbies like cooking, sport, gardening, winning awards, or even travelling to new places, are the achievements you realise in self-actualization. This is the point at which you are at the peak of your life.

Peak experiences are transcendent moments in life, filled with elation and pure joy. These moments are unique, and their memories are uplifting. They are characterised by deep feelings and intense perceptions, and carry a sense of profound significance. Remember when we talked about self-actualization as fulfilling your creative, social, and intellectual potential? This is the apex.

A self-actualised person is unshakable. You accept yourself as you are, flawed, unashamed by individual quirks, and at the same time, accept and embrace others as you do yourself. You are purpose-driven and have clear missions in life, which you pursue with a sense of duty and responsibility.

You cannot achieve self-actualization without self-discipline. The very definition of self-actualization speaks volumes about the level of discipline required for success. Self-awareness, learning to stay in control of situations instead of being controlled by them, not acting on impulse; these are prerequisites to overcoming obstacles in life. This is how you get unstuck from the hamster wheel of life and rush towards your potential.

Importance of Self-Discipline

The key to success in life is self-discipline. Life is full of obstacles and distractions that constantly threaten your pursuit of success. Why and how is self-discipline the all-important ingredient in your life? You must instil discipline in yourself to get that unstoppable force that pushes you to the greatest level in life. Below are some reasons explaining the value of self-discipline to your success:

1. Humans are Habitual Creatures

Habits will make or break you—that's just human nature. You are your thoughts, beliefs, and actions. These are the things that define who you are and influence your core values. Through self-discipline, you create good habits that are aligned with your success goals. You know a lot of people who are ill-disciplined and lazy. Laziness is also a habit.

The difference is that successful people choose not to be lazy, and that's where discipline comes in. You discipline yourself to work hard and consistently commit to delivering results. This persistence creates a habit, and as you get used to it, success will certainly follow you.

2. Builds Commitment

You must be disciplined to overcome distractions and get things done. This doesn't necessarily have to be on grandiose things. Usually, it's the small things that make the biggest difference. You see, life is about compounding effort. In everything you do, small but consistent attempts eventually build into something big. The discipline comes in the commitment to complete what you start.

Commitment to never leaving things pending soon becomes a habit, and eventually a culture. This becomes your personality. You don't start anything you won't finish, and with this culture, you can easily become a high achiever in life. Self-discipline helps you create a culture of commitment and consistency, and you can achieve anything in life with that kind of persistence.

3. Helps You Focus

Self-discipline can help you overcome distractions and stay focused on your goals. You stick to what you are supposed to do because you know what it means to your overall success. If you are focused on your goals, you will accomplish every task necessary. This laser-sharp focus is what makes the difference between successful people and everyone else.

4. Work Ethics

Ever wondered how successful people have such an amazing work acumen? It comes down to self-discipline. Successful people believe in themselves, and even though you might not see it, they work harder than everyone else. This kind of work ethic is also what makes them good leaders. They lead by example, and to do this they must be good at what they do. They don't just teach, they coach. They empower people around them.

Such traits not only show how serious you are about your work, but they also boost your self-esteem. Being disciplined boosts your work ethic, helps you achieve objectives, and feel confident about yourself and your work. This is why discipline is mandatory for success.

5. Become a Better Person

You must be good at something to succeed at it. Whether you are trained or not, mastery comes from spending countless hours refining your skills. You can only commit so many hours to something with discipline. One of the reasons why many people fail is because they don't spend enough time perfecting their skills. They rush over everything, trying to learn a lot of things at the same time.

Mastery comes from picking one thing, learning everything about it, and how to be the best at it. Even when you eventually succeed, you still look for ways to keep refining what you are already good at. This kind of expertise requires an insane level of commitment, professionalism, and discipline.

The thing about self-discipline is that as you work towards greatness, you experience wholesome growth too. You don't just become a master at your skills, career, and anything else you are working on, you also become a better, refined version of yourself. Subtle but consistent improvements will also improve your attitude and personality, and eventually, you succeed because you truly deserve it, and everyone around you knows it. Self-discipline breeds personal improvement, making you a better person every day, and this is why it is mandatory for a lifetime of growth and success.

Resilience in Self-Discipline

Unresolved spiritual and emotional baggage is often responsible for the disconnected life that many people live. It's difficult to forge ahead in life if you constantly think about the past and other things that you cannot change. This is what holds you back, and most of the time, you might not even know you are in pain or recognise what you feel until it becomes such big a problem your behaviour and attitudes change.

While we all want to succeed and be the best version of ourselves, the ability, skill, and strength necessary to achieve this do not come naturally to everyone. Your ambition notwithstanding, success is difficult, and the more you pursue it, the more the grind can weigh heavily on your emotional, mental, and physical health.

The path to success is lined with struggle, so much that at times it almost is easier to give up. High performers and achievers all face these challenges, yet somehow, they overcome them. Discouragement, fatigue, burnout, failure, stress, delimiting beliefs, and self-doubt are obstacles you have to overcome to succeed, yet this isn't even an exhaustive list of challenges. How is it that some people consistently pursue and achieve their personal and professional goals every year, yet others don't? How do they persevere and stay strong when everything in life is practically wired against them? Simple answer—mental strength!

Like self-discipline, mental strength is critical to success. Talent alone can only get you so far. Talent, persistence, and passion, on the other hand, will carry you all the way. The core of mental toughness is to get tougher as the going gets tough. This is why high achievers succeed while everyone else abandons their dreams.

Well, you should know that there is always time to turn your life around. You can develop mental toughness and regain control of your life. Let's discuss simple steps to get you there:

1. Positive Outlook

At times we struggle to find a way out of situations because of perspective. Change is everywhere in life and you have to embrace it. It's amazing the kind of changes you can make in life by adopting a different perspective. A positive mindset can help you look at things a different way, and even find a solution where you never thought one was feasible.

Do not hold onto delimiting beliefs—perceived boundaries in your life whose unfortunate effect is to hold you back and prevent you from realizing your true potential. Life and the struggles within are hard enough, you don't need to put yourself down too. We face challenges all the time, and just because the challenge seems insurmountable, does not mean it actually is. Try something different, talk to someone about it. Here's my favourite—take a breather and do something else, then come back to it later. This usually helps.

You've probably told yourself the following statements more than enough times:

> *'I tried that before, it didn't work.'*
>
> *'Maybe I'm not cut out for this.'*
>
> *'I don't think I have what it takes.'*
>
> *'What will they think about me?'*

You might not realise it, but such statements go a long way, and the longer you have them flooding your mind, the easier it is to believe them as your truth. Challenge these thoughts. So what if you tried something the first time, second time, or fifth time, and it didn't work. That's not a guarantee that it will fail this time.

Mental strength is not always about how strong or how brave you are. At times, all that matters is how well you can utilise whatever little strength you have in you. The beauty of this is not just how it keeps you going, but in realizing how much you can achieve by believing in yourself, and applying the last ounce of energy or courage you have left.

Look around, all the great personalities you know today have probably gone through many experiences where they thought they would never make it. If you can change your mindset, nothing will stand in your way. You will approach challenges with a renewed sense of determination. This fortitude is what breeds greatness.

2. Lessons from Failure

You learn more in failure than you will ever learn in success. Failure is a normal experience in life—you probably have experienced your fair share by now. Obstacles, failure, and setbacks are inevitable on your way to success. Failure can be heartbreaking, but the lessons you learn from it will strengthen your resolve.

Even though you try to be positive about disappointment, you must also admit and face the reality. Do not be in denial about failure, accept it for what it is. Things didn't work out. Perhaps you miscalculated some steps or underestimated the opponent. After a disappointment, go back to the drawing board and review your process. Therein, you will find the answers you seek.

Learning from your mistakes can build your resilience. Ask yourself the difficult questions, for example:

> *'Is this project still worth pursuing?'*
>
> *'Can I get a different opinion on this?'*
>
> *'Do I need to take a break?'*
>
> *'What positives can I learn from this?'*

At a cursory glance, these might seem like normal, simple questions. However, what you don't realise is that they help you check your mindset. You can get lost wallowing in the failure such that you feel you've lost your purpose or your connection to the ultimate goals.

This is not true. It takes a lot of self-discipline and mental strength to review your failure and learn from it. When you get used to this process, you will never be afraid to fail. Instead, you will welcome challenges as opportunities to conquer the unknown.

3. Ditch Unhealthy Comparisons

We waste a lot of time comparing ourselves to other people. Whatever your position in life, there's always going to be someone doing better, or who has achieved greater things. You can get so caught up in the pursuit of success that you lose the plot. Do not compare yourself with others—this is easier said than done. Indeed, someone will drive by with a better car, own a bigger house, share a dinner table with people you've always wished you could know. None of these things takes away anything from your success or your struggle.

Your identity is unique. What you might not realise is that as you beat yourself up for not having or achieving what someone else has, there's someone who probably wishes they had what you have. In their opinion, you already have it all.

Comparison robs you the opportunity to enjoy what you have: your wins, successes, everything. Make the most of who you are and what you have. If someone rubs their success in your face, congratulate them and wish them well. You are running a different race. If you feel it's necessary to make some changes in your life, go ahead. However, do it for you, not because someone else did it. As long as you are alive, the world will never run out of happier, richer, better people or at the very least, those who are not, but create a perfect illusion of it. Focus on you, do you.

4. Appreciate Small Wins

When we talk about resilience and mental strength, we are talking about the end result. The fortitude, the grit, everything, that's the end result. The important question is, how did you get there? We get caught up chasing the big wins, we forget that they come from small wins. A series of small wins creates more momentum than one big win.

Considering everything you want to achieve in life, you must get excited about the small wins. Coming from a point of procrastination, inability to control your emotions, or lack of confidence to being the finest version of yourself is no mean feat. You don't just wake up one day and become a different person. You make subtle, consistent changes and commit to the end result.

Life is like raising a baby. You learn new things every day, and each lesson helps you develop and become the amazing person you want to be. Sure, you will fall a few times, but you will still get up and continue the journey. Appreciate the small things you accomplish, and the interactions and connections you make therein.

More often, you spend more time worrying about how much more work you need to do, how much farther you have to go, that you forget about everything you have achieved so far. It takes time to build mental strength. It gets easier, however, with practice.

Resilience is important in self-discipline. There are more ways to increase your mental strength than we can cover in this book. We've looked at simple things that are evident in your immediate surroundings—which you can work on—and create the perfect foundation for a rejuvenated life. What's more important in this journey is how much you are aware of where you are heading in life, where you are, and who you are.

An important lesson in developing mental toughness is awareness of your negative traits and tendencies, and committing to changing them. Change the negative feelings, thoughts, and behaviours with healthy ones. The name notwithstanding, mental toughness is not necessarily about gaining strength and eliminating weakness. The crux of it is learning your weaknesses, embracing them, and overcoming them.

Other than acceptance and awareness, you will also realise that while you cannot control everything that happens around you, you have something greater, much better—control over your reaction and response to it. There's no greater power than being in control of your mind. It might take a while to train your mind, and lots of effort and commitment, but the long-term results are wholesome and you will live a satisfying life. Better relationships, performance, an amazing sense of well-being, self-discipline; all this is possible. It all starts with training your mind.

Steps to Achieving Your Goals

Remember how you work hard to build muscle? You need the same intentional exercise routines to help you develop self-discipline, a function of your mental muscle. You can build self-discipline through the following simple routines:

1. Accept Your Reality

Ignorance can only get you so far, and it never changes your reality. You must first recognise and acknowledge your weaknesses. This is your reality. Identify some of your quirks. It could be procrastination, cookie cravings that hamper your weight loss goals, or spending too much time on social media, affecting your productivity. The most important step in driving change is to recognise your weaknesses.

2. Plan of Action

Building from the point above, come up with a clear plan of action. You can't wake up one day, flip a switch, and turn things around. Developing self-discipline takes time. How do you turn your good intentions into actionable plans? What steps will you take, even subtle, to change your reality?

3. Eliminate Temptations

The next step to building self-discipline is to remove the stumbling blocks from your environment. If your goal is to eat healthily and lose weight, for example, a house stocked with cookies and junk food will undermine your efforts. Remove all unhealthy snacks from the house. This will not just make it easier to eat healthily, but it will also send a message to your brain; change is imminent, and it must adapt. You build self-discipline over time by identifying and eliminating such distractions.

4. Embrace Change

More often, change is uncomfortable. The desire for a comfortable life means that you are naturally inclined to pursue ways of avoiding pain. However, to build your self-discipline, you should learn to tolerate discomfort from time to time. Each time you avoid pain, you teach your mind that you are incapable of handling stress. Change is inevitable, and by embracing it, you prove to yourself that you have enough strength to handle it.

5. Visualization

Think of all the things you have been unable to accomplish for lack of self-discipline. Think of what you can achieve if you stay the course. Visualise your goals and the transformative impact of self-discipline. Go a step further and list everything you can achieve if you diligently stick to your plans and resist the temptation to give up. Let that good feeling motivate and drive you to turn your life around.

The key to a better life is to boost your self-control. With a bit of training on mental toughness, you can build your resilience and willpower. The best thing about the journey you are embarking on is that improving self-discipline in one area of your life can trigger similar changes in other aspects of your life too.

CHAPTER TWO

The Enemy Within

At one point in life, everyone has fallen victim to procrastination. Avoiding or delaying action on something important to you are challenges that have been around for as long as the human race has existed. When you experience momentary bursts of production, you temporarily realise how much time you have wasted, and even think of how you can stop procrastination. But, have you ever wondered why you procrastinate? I mean, the things you are supposed to do are clear, and you know why you should do them, yet you still never do. What goes on in the brain to stop you from doing what you should?

The science of procrastination points us to a concept known as time inconsistency. This is the tendency of your brain to prefer immediate rewards over future rewards. This explains why you might go to sleep feeling excited and motivated about turning your life around, but when you wake up in the morning, you slip right back into your old patterns. The brain values instant gratification more than future long-term benefits.

Procrastination is one of the obstacles preventing you from making the right decisions or living the life you have always wanted. Procrastination doesn't just steal your time, it also steals your joy. This is because people generally feel bad about things they did not accomplish. The guilt and regret that comes from realizing the impact or effect of procrastination can stay with you for a long time, eroding your happiness.

While procrastination might feel like it at times, it is not laziness. Putting off things until the very last moment does not mean you are lazy. A lazy person simply won't do anything and is okay not doing anything. A procrastinator, on the other hand, wants to do something and probably has the desire to do it, but cannot find that urge to start.

On the same note, you must also not confuse procrastination with relaxation. Procrastination drains your energy, while relaxing allows your body to recollect and rejuvenate, coming back energised. Many times we try to validate procrastination as being able to work best when under pressure. This is a common excuse people give to put things off until the last minute. The only thing you can achieve from this is setting the foundation for guilt, stress, and ineffectiveness.

How Procrastination Creeps In

Procrastination is the easiest example of self-sabotage. To work your way out of it, it's important to understand where you are coming from. Why do you procrastinate, despite your best efforts to stop? The reasons below can help you identify why you procrastinate, and from there, build on to tackle the challenges:

1. Creative Confusion

A common misconception about procrastination is that you are just not creative enough. What you might not realise is that procrastination might be feeding on your creativity. This is common in people who have a lot of amazing ideas bursting through their heads. Having too many ideas without order creates confusion since you cannot find a way to organise and execute them.

This kind of confusion points to a lack of structure. It's like waking up in the morning fully aware that you have a lot of things to do, but without creating a to-do list, you probably spend more time than you should on other tasks or none at all.

This can also point to a deficiency in goal setting. You might have a lot of ideas, but without setting an agenda or strategy, you go about the relevant tasks aimlessly. The problem with this approach is that you will delay decision-making, hence having disproportionate time allocation on tasks. Eventually, your greater objective is delayed too.

The simplest way around this is to organise yourself. If you have a lot of things to do, or brilliant ideas in your creative mind, write them down and plan a timeline for them. Set objectives for what to achieve and assign timelines to them. Ideally, you are setting the blueprints for accountability, and you will also stay on track.

One of the biggest challenges that creatives experience is bouncing from one idea or concept to the other. You believe that you can accomplish so much in a short time. Unfortunately, you spread yourself too thin and you don't achieve anything. Your energy is drained from all the pressure and realizing that you did not accomplish anything despite your best efforts. You can easily slump into depression because of this. With all the ideas or things to do, the best solution is to find ways of cultivating focus.

2. Fear of Failure

If you are afraid of failure, it is easier to put off something until a later date, hoping that by then, you will have overcome that fear. This is a subconscious decision that takes place in your brain without your realization. The same applies to people who are obsessed with the finest details. You worry about everything falling in place the way you visualised it in your mind. This can be overwhelming, making you shelve the task for a later time when you feel comfortable.

Each of these situations is perpetuated by fear. Your desire to forge ahead is impeded by your fear of things or circumstances whose existence you might not be able to prove yet. This fear is driven by the pursuit of perfection. To be fair, no one is perfect. Perfection is a fallacy and instead of dwelling on it, do your best and appreciate the effort and commitment.

3. Giving in to Distractions

Distraction is probably one of the common reasons why people procrastinate. People have different concentration levels. If your brain cannot concentrate on something for a long time, it will certainly divert your attention to something else. Throw in the modern environment that is full of escape outlets, like so many interesting topics you can delve into with your chatty mates, or immersing yourself in social media. Before you realise it, the day is gone and you haven't accomplished anything.

The thing about distraction is that at times, it might not be about self-sabotage. At times you are an innocent victim of circumstances. Perhaps you are in an environment where it's impossible to ignore the distractions.

To overcome distractions, you must first study and understand your environment. recognise the potential distractions and how you can avoid them. If your biggest problem is chatty workmates, plug in some headphones to get in the zone. You are less distracted when you can't be part of the conversation.

Whether you procrastinate as a result of the environment around you or self-sabotage, you are always in control. You can make an independent decision to block out distractions. Worried about spending too much time on your phone? Turn it off until you finish your tasks. If you operate in a busy environment, schedule small breaks after every burst of productivity. Give yourself some 20-30 minutes between tasks to relax and rejuvenate.

4. Lack of Priorities

Almost similar to the point about creative confusion, you might be a procrastinator because you cannot organise your tasks accordingly. This is possible because you have too many things on your to-do list, or perhaps you don't understand the varying levels of importance you should assign to each task. The result is chaos and confusion, and you won't get anything done.

Without setting priorities, you spend most of your time switching between tasks, hoping that you will eventually complete them. You might also waste a lot of time planning or thinking of what to do, without doing the deed. This is a common problem for multitaskers.

Multitasking has often been a conundrum in that while some people swear by it, it might be a sign of disorganization. If you carefully analyse the situations where you multitask, you will realise that in most cases, you never have to get to that point. A few moments earlier, you could have done everything in its allocated time. With so much to accomplish in a short time, you can mix things up, forget important details, and fail at setting priorities.

The need for priorities means you realise the urgency or importance of some tasks over others. Create a list based on this realization. Review the tasks before you in terms of their purpose and value. With so much to do in the office, for example, checking and responding to emails every few minutes will rob you of precious time. Set a time for the emails and focus on other priorities. Besides, if a colleague sends you an urgent email and they don't get a response as fast as they expected, they can call your extension and request you to have a look at it.

5. Overwhelming Avoidance

Procrastination might also creep in because you are overwhelmed. Thinking of the task or challenge ahead can make you lose concentration and motivation. You might end up pushing the task too far ahead and avoid doing it altogether. You take solace in the awesomeness of the comfort zone.

Note, however, that you are willing to put in the work, just not on the difficult tasks. Instead, you look for simpler tasks that you consider more enjoyable, putting off the rest. Unfortunately, the cycle comes to an end and once the simple tasks are completed, you are left with the difficult ones that you dread. Stress sets in when you realise that you must still complete the tasks.

This is a common challenge many people experience. Break down tasks that seem insurmountable. Breaking them into smaller assignments makes it easier to tackle them one by one. Apart from making difficult tasks manageable, you might also realise that the solution was simpler than you had earlier imagined. It's always advisable to start your day with difficult tasks. Accomplishing them early gives you the momentum that sets the tone for the rest of the day.

The Negative Impact

The activity you are unable to accomplish doesn't create procrastination, you do. The impact of procrastination can be anything from missing an opportunity to missing an important deadline. If you are lucky, you can identify and stop procrastination in time before it ruins your life. Others are not that lucky and have to live with the long-term consequences of procrastination for the rest of their lives.

Your reason for procrastination might be different from the next person, and at times the reason might not be so apparent. Whether it's for lack of motivation or hidden fear, the only person who can understand and change the course of your life is you. Procrastination generally happens in any of the following ways:

1. You don't start your tasks at all.
2. You postpone important decisions if you feel they need more information than you are prepared to process.
3. You don't finish tasks or take longer to complete them.

Whatever your reasons might be, or how it manifests, you can slide into chronic procrastination without realizing it, and the long-term effects can mess up your life. Here are some of the negative effects of procrastination, and how they might ruin your life:

1. Chronic Failure

There's always that urge to take a step back and relax a bit immediately when you think of your goals, or if you want to change something. At this point, your desire to work on your goals is defeated by the inability to take the first step.

The problem with such a situation is that it is usually confusing, because on one hand, you have a strong desire to achieve something, but on the other, you are too reluctant to start. How can it be so hard to pursue something that you want so badly?

The whole point behind setting goals is to accomplish something, and in the process, improve your life. Since you are unable to set and commit to your goals, you limit your chances of success, and might even set yourself up for failure.

2. Effect on Your Reputation

The problem with persistent procrastination is that it creates a reputation for you; a bad one. If you keep making and breaking promises, you gain a reputation for being that empty promise colleague, parent, or friend. Procrastination won't stop at your reputation. It will soon erode your self-confidence and esteem, and since you are no longer surprised by your delaying tactics anymore, you go deeper down the procrastination rabbit hole because it is easier than trying to prove to yourself and others that you are better than that.

With time, people give up on you and no one depends on you. Since you are not dependable, people hold back and don't send opportunities your way because they are afraid of cleaning up after your mess.

3. Erodes Your Self-Esteem

Procrastination perpetuates a vicious cycle that will not just erode your self-esteem but can steal every bit of joy in your life. It lowers your self-esteem because you feel inadequate and unable to commit to the project in the right way, or get it done on time. If you are already suffering from low self-esteem and confidence, procrastination will feed on your fears and insecurities, making you doubt yourself further.

The problem with low self-esteem is that it makes you hold back, and doubt your talent and abilities. You feel you are so unworthy, you don't deserve success, and with time, self-sabotage sets in. Procrastination worsens these feelings.

4. Mental Health Concerns

Stress and anxiety are normal experiences you go through in life. The magnitude of each situation is different, as are your responses to them. Procrastination can exacerbate the situation, resulting in mental health problems.

You might experience anxiety or feelings of depression when you realise that you are constantly lagging behind because of procrastination. The other challenge with procrastination is that you usually know what you are supposed to do, and when you suffer the consequences, you can look back and identify where you lost the plot. This realization comes with regret, disappointment, and resentment, and the negative vibes can spill over into other parts of your life.

Besides, if you constantly procrastinate about a task, you will soon start stressing over it, especially when you have to collaborate with other people. You worry that they might realise you are a burden, or you have imposter syndrome. These feelings take a toll on you and affect your health.

If you've gotten away with putting off tasks until a later date, what's to stop you from putting off routine exercise, medical checkups, and appointments? In the long run, your reality will have more dire consequences.

5. Missed Opportunities

You waste a lot of time through procrastination. What starts as ignoring your work for a few hours soon turns into days, and before you know it, a few years have gone and you are still stuck in the same place. By this time, everyone around you has moved on to greater things and taken bigger, more demanding roles, and you can easily point to the growth trajectory in their life. You, on the other hand, are stagnant and have nothing to show for all the time you have been there.

Unfortunately, you cannot turn back the hands of time, and the terrible reality is that you must live with the consequences of your actions, which includes a lot of regrets. This situation is frustrating because you know that all you had to do was take that first step a few years back, and your life would be different. You missed your golden opportunity and must now be content with living a subordinate life.

Think about it for a moment, how many opportunities have passed you by because you couldn't take a leap of faith? List them down, go through them, and see how long it will take before you feel you deserve a punch in the gut. Many life-changing opportunities can pass you by while you wait on the sidelines. Such opportunities only come once, and if you don't take them up, someone else will. Why would you let go of your destiny like that?

6. Ruined Careers

Procrastination has not only ruined careers, but it's also ended many. Every corporate workspace has the classic procrastination story from time to time. An individual joins the team, energetic, ambitious, and excited at the prospect of the amazing opportunities that lie ahead. However, what was once an individual with a promising future turns into a consistent record of failure.

Your work ethics affect your results directly. They determine your performance and achievements and your long-term position. The cost of procrastination might be too steep; it takes away everything you've worked so hard to build.

The moment you start missing deadlines and targets, the only constant in your life becomes underachievement. It won't be long before the company decides it's in their best interest to replace you. Remember that companies are run as going concerns, and your role is clearly outlined in your job description. If you can't live up to expectations, there's hundreds, thousands, or even millions of other people out there who can replace you.

At first, the effect of procrastination might not seem so dire, but their compounding impact on your life will finish you. Think of broken dreams, anxiety, stress, and eroded self-esteem, and you will see how your life might spiral out of control.

Going through the negative effects of procrastination, it is evident that in the worst possible scenario, you could lose everything. What's the solution? Take action! Instead of pushing it aside, do something right away. Start, even in the smallest way, just start and get going. This will motivate you, and before long, you will complete the task. Taking action might not be as easy as we make it out to be, so let's look at simple ways you can wrest your life back from procrastination.

Winning Your Life Back

There's a good chance that you are procrastinating on something at this very moment. Perhaps, you might even be reading this book to do so. Procrastination can seem harmless from time to time, but what you don't realise is that when you add up all the time you wasted, you lost a huge chunk of your life. How do you overcome procrastination without hating yourself or the methods used in the process? Now that you've learned how to conquer the enemy within, let's go on and win your life back.

1. Fight Fire with Fire

Fair warning, though the concept is clear, this might be a difficult one, and it needs a lot of discipline to hack. It is easy to procrastinate on a task if you feel that it is boring, frustrating, ambiguous, difficult, or lacks structure. The same applies to tasks that you struggle to attach personal meaning to or something that, simply put, you don't feel is rewarding.

The challenge with procrastination is that it is more emotional than logical. When you choose to catch up on the latest adventures of Ragnar Lothbrok's sons in Vikings instead of writing that Literature Review chapter in your term paper, the logical part of your brain (prefrontal cortex) surrenders control to the emotional part (limbic system).

So in essence, procrastination is about feelings,

which takes us back to the earlier statement. You feel the task is boring, frustrating, ambiguous, and so on. At this point, all logic is gone. So, how do you fight fire with fire? Consider that ill-feeling you have towards a task. For example, let's say you feel the task is boring. Try to think about it in a different light and make completing the task more appealing.

That Literature Review might be a difficult chapter to write, but you can switch things up a bit. Create a game out of it or a reward system. Challenge yourself to work on it uninterrupted for 30 minutes. Set a target, perhaps 500 words. If you beat that target, reward yourself with something exciting. The idea here is to dig deeper into the feelings behind procrastination and reverse them.

2. Opportunity Cost of Procrastination

Opportunity cost is a financial concept that refers to the cost in terms of the best foregone alternative (Fagan, 2020). In simpler terms, what you stand to lose by choosing an alternative, which in our case is whatever you are doing instead of what you should be doing. For example, if you have two hours to spend and you go to the movies, the time and money spent going to the movies is gone, and cannot be redeemed on something else, like finishing your term paper.

Write a list of what procrastination will cost you. This is a good idea, especially if you are struggling with big tasks. What does this mean? Of course, it might not make sense spending 30 minutes to write a list of the opportunity cost of skipping your morning run for a few more minutes of sleep. However, that retirement savings plan, getting medical insurance, seeing a therapist, or moving out of mom's nest, are examples of big decisions you might be pushing aside. Note down every benefit or impact foregone by maintaining the status quo. This might include effects on your happiness, stress, finances, social life, health, employment, career advancement, and so on.

This list can be the wake-up call you need. The thing about life is that it goes on. Whether you use your time wisely or not, life waits for no one. Every opportunity you lose to procrastination is a chance you'll never get back. Look at your list of missed opportunities, and think of your reasons for procrastination—is it worth it?

3. Identify Distractions

While advancement in technology is amazing, it also comes with challenges in the form of distractions. Everywhere you turn these days, there's always something screaming for your attention. Whether it's social media, your email, a new movie, a new video on YouTube, a notification on your phone, you name it. Even friends and family members have become distractions. Your work becomes more unstructured and ambiguous the longer you entertain such distractions.

The secret is to identify these distractions and disconnect from them. For example, if your phone is the problem, put it in silent mode in one room and get busy in the other. If you are struggling to focus because of notifications or anything else online, turn off your wireless network and work. Luckily, today we even have apps that you can use to disconnect and focus on what's important.

4. Set Targets

Everyone talks about commitment to a cause. Is there anything in your life you are religiously committed to? How is that working for you? The thing about causes is that before commitment, there must be a target or goals. This simply answers the question '*What are you working towards?*'

Setting targets is one way of fighting procrastination. The beauty of this approach is that you are not limited by the size of your objective. Whether it's a task as simple as your regular morning run or competing in the triathlon, a working target gives you a sense of direction. This is how motivation comes in, and you get things done.

It's also safe to mention that your targets should be realistic. If you've never driven a car in your life, for example, don't expect to walk into an airport and fly a plane in a month, all protocols notwithstanding. Okay, let's bring it closer home...if you have ignored your research paper throughout the term, don't expect you'll write it in a day and get good grades. That is setting yourself up for disappointment.

Set yourself a realistic target. If you have five chapters to write, commit to writing one chapter every week. From there, look at your schedule for the week and decide how many words you will write each day. These are realistic and achievable targets and will help you across the bridge and stop procrastination.

There are more strategies you can use to fight procrastination, each unique to the situation at hand. You'll realise that most of them borrow from the four concepts we discussed above in one way or the other. Use whichever strategy you can, as long as it helps you stop procrastinating. Procrastination isn't something debilitating or crippling that you must live with all your life.

The fact that it is mostly triggered as an emotional response to your obligation means a change of attitude can go a long way. With the right resources and attitude, you can conquer it and get your life back on track. Dedicate yourself to beating it, set realistic goals that can keep you motivated, and you'll see the results very soon. Remember, as long as you stay the course, even the slightest positive change in your attitude can go a long way.

CHAPTER
THREE

Focus and Live the Life You Want

One of the constants in life is change. To live the life you want, you must embrace change from time to time. It is the prerequisite for personal development. Embracing change is how you get to improve yourself and live a better life, the life you want. To achieve this, you must also learn to set targets and focus on how and when to achieve them.

This type of self-improvement is important to your happiness, but unfortunately, is something that most people never give priority to in their lives. To live a fulfilling life, you must focus on yourself, your personal growth and your development in every aspect, from your personal life, education and career.

The beauty of life is that whether you accept it or not, change happens all the time. With changing circumstances, you find yourself in situations where you need a new motivation to keep going. To understand this idea better, let's look at some reasons why personal development should be a priority, and the impact it can have on your well-being and happiness in general:

1. Self-Esteem and Confidence

There's an incredible sense of achievement that fills you each time you accomplish your goals. It doesn't matter how small or big they are, the fact that you beat the odds and crossed the finish line emboldens you. This becomes the beginning of many great things to come. Every accomplishment becomes a reminder that all you have to do is put your mind to something and you will get it done. This is the kind of belief that gives you a confidence boost and works wonders for your self-esteem.

Why is this important? Most often, you can be your worst enemy, second-guessing your every move, skills, and abilities. By setting goals and focusing on them, you develop your knowledge, push your limits, and pursue challenges that you would have otherwise ignored altogether. Identify those areas of your life that you are not confident about and do something about them. The ripple effect will be great for your life in general.

2. Career Growth

What are your career goals? When we talk of career growth, most people limit their ideology to taking classes, moving from one company to the other, and so on. While this growth trajectory might be good for your career, personal development is even more important. There is more to career progression than courses and promotions. Other elements, like learning new skills and accepting new challenges at work, will get you that recognition.

Employers value team members with initiative, who are motivated and rise to the challenge whenever they are called upon. Your willingness to learn is a great way to show your dedication and commitment to the cause. In the long run, you get the best of professional and personal development.

3. Being a Better Person

You become a better person by improving on your weaknesses and building on your strengths. There are many ways to go about this in every sphere of your life. Accepting new challenges is not limited to a professional career. Challenges are available all over the place. Each obstacle you overcome helps to build your character.

What are your weaknesses or strengths? If you can identify them, list them down. If not, talk to someone who knows or understands you better to write that list for you. A cursory glance at that list can reveal areas where you need to improve. That is the simplest way to set personal growth and development goals. Remember that improving soft skills like communication can have quite a transformative impact on your life too.

4. Exiting the Comfort Zone

The comfort zone is one of the most mentioned subjects in the self-help realm. It is quite a paradox because losing yourself in the comfort zone can make your life quite uncomfortable and unbearable. Your comfort zone is all but an illusion of accomplishment, greatness, and everything else that you feel you might have achieved. A common saying sums it up perfectly, that life begins at the end of your comfort zone.

Slumping into a comfort zone holds you back from taking up opportunities that might come your way. In the process, it denies you the chance of experiencing true success. You can find yourself in a comfort zone for any manner of reasons. Many people get comfortable when they are ahead and winning. The problem with being ahead for so long is that you might never realise when the game has changed behind you. Before you know it, you are obsolete.

To avoid this predicament, set goals that push you outside your comfort zone. Usually, you have to think outside the box and do the extraordinary to achieve such goals. You will be surprised when you achieve things you never thought were possible, and that's how you experience true growth.

5. Wholesome Personal Growth

If there's one lesson you will learn about personal development that should stay with you forever, it is that you are responsible for yourself. Everything you want, from personal development to career progression, is a personal choice. No one will do it for you. No one can make you learn a new skill. Everything you achieve is out of personal initiative. Thus, it's safe to say that the only person stopping you from achieving greatness is you.

With this in mind, you should prioritise self-improvement, otherwise, you'll find yourself living a mediocre life. Everyone has a different definition of success. While one person's idea of success is to become a director in one of the top companies, another's concept might be making enough money to assist the less fortunate in their community. Once you set your sights on what you want to achieve and commit to it, nothing can stand in your way.

The beauty of striving for self-improvement and living life on your terms is that you become a better, happier person with each accomplishment. To live your best life, you must always constantly challenge yourself to do better.

Stop Lying to Yourself

When you think of the reasons why you might not be realizing your personal goals, it's easy to point out things that most people can easily identify, for example, spending too much time on things that don't matter, procrastination, or disinterest in something. However, what you might not realise is that the biggest obstacle lies in your mind, in the form of the lies you tell yourself from time to time.

You're probably wondering, *'How is that even possible?'*, right? *'How can I lie to myself?'*

It's true. We tell ourselves a few lies from time to time to feel comfortable about the progress we are making in life. This is how you get away with doing nothing. For example, let's say you want to read a book. You've been stuck on one page for hours on end, and in between, flipped through your phone, watched a movie, and done everything else apart from reading that book. When someone asks, you claim you've been reading the book, but in reality, you know you've barely flipped a page.

What happens, in this case, is that you avoid taking responsibility and being accountable for the lack of commitment. After all, no one is around to hold you accountable. The lie is further perpetuated by flimsy excuses like *'My mind just isn't in the right place right now.'* or *'I will find time tomorrow and read a few more chapters'*.

From this assessment, you realise that each of the statements is geared towards making you feel better, yet you haven't achieved any of your goals. So, why would you feel so entitled to a sense of accomplishment, when in the real sense, you're not making any progress?

The thing about these soft lies we tell ourselves is that they give you a way out of self-awareness. Deep down, you know there isn't much progress going on, but you need the feelings and emotions to track progress. What happens is that you end up lying to yourself about what's really going on.

If you want to make progress in something important, you must perform a self-audit and understand where you are. This level of self-awareness is one of the most important steps towards self-improvement. Using our example above, how do you go about this?

Well, first you have to accept that you haven't been reading. You need an element of structure to see this through. Why not commit to reading one or two chapters a day? That makes more sense because you know where to start and stop, and more importantly, you know you must accomplish it daily. With such simple measures, you can track progress over time. This kind of structure gives you a measure of performance and strengthens your commitment to the cause.

Unless you are aware of what you are doing, it's almost impossible to change anything in your life or institute an element of consistency. Building better habits to help you focus and live the life you want is almost inconceivable without self-awareness. It's like someone spinning you around blindfolded, and then asking you to hit the bullseye.

Small, consistent measures of accountability go a long way. While you started by reading one or two chapters a day, with time you realise that the only way to achieve this target is to schedule quiet reading time in your day. It soon becomes a thing, almost second nature to you. This kind of structure helps you get in touch with your reality. Once you become fully aware of what's going on in your life, what you want to achieve, what you are not doing right, what you can do to make things better, you have a means of measuring progress. With time, this self-awareness can heighten your gut feeling, helping you make accurate decisions without referring to the structures in place.

Remember, if nothing changes, nothing is going to change!

Staying Calm in a Storm

Chaos is almost inevitable in life, everyone experiences it in some form from time to time. Its nature and severity might vary from one person to the next, but in most cases, chaos is almost always preceded by moments of difficulty or tough circumstances in life. It could be a failed relationship, life-threatening disease, unexpected news, or anything else that disrupts your balance. Even moments of extreme happiness can create chaos in your life.

Chaotic moments in life detract you from focusing on your goals. They consume your time and energy. You spend most of your time putting out fires in your life or being caught up in the thrill of the good times. Chaos sucks. More often, it's easier to ignore things and hope that life will balance itself out, but that never happens.

Life unravels so fast today. There are endless opportunities everywhere you turn, yet instead of feeling stimulated, motivated, and energised to take them, most people complain about how overwhelmed they are. The challenge here is that instead of living the life you want, you get caught up in the chaos, and live the life that's handed to you. You give up control over your life to any person, situation, experience, or circumstance you encounter. Instead of managing and overcoming the chaos in your life, you make peace with it. It becomes a part of you—your new normal. Let's look at some simple strategies to stay calm, overcome chaotic experiences, and regain your focus:

1. Understand Processes

Recognise the process of dealing with every disruptive occurrence in life, and learn how to manage them. For example, let's say you are grappling with an uncomfortable situation like a business failure or any kind of personal loss. In its wake, a sense of uncertainty might creep in. Uncertainty breeds discomfort. It might take you a while to understand the situation and embrace your new reality. With time, you gain better insight into the situation, understand why or how it happened, and find a way to move past it, or integrate its impact into your life.

Given the difference in personality traits and experiences, each of these stages unravels differently for everyone. For example, someone with a strong support system will usually process and overcome chaos faster and better than someone who doesn't and who might feel isolated or downtrodden when such things happen.

Think of similar experiences in the past and reflect on how you handled them. While each circumstance might be unique, and probably not as difficult as what you are going through right now, take pride in the fact that you made it. You are in this present moment because you could overcome those challenges.

Knowledge of these transitions makes it easier to get through anything, manage the chaos, and regain focus on your personal goals. This is true, because when uncertainty sets in, the discomfort doesn't overwhelm you. You expect it, embrace it, and use it to gain more insight into your situation.

2. Managing Your Resources

We all have the same 24 hours, yet some people seem to do more with theirs than others. Time is another crucial factor in managing chaos in your life. When things are difficult, most people worry about how to manage their time, and this is where they go wrong. Indeed, time management is a good skill. However, you cannot control time. Instead, you can control your energy.

Knowing how your energy levels fluctuate throughout the day, schedule tasks accordingly. Do the difficult tasks when you feel energised. Accomplishing such tasks will motivate you to keep going. This is probably the best time to schedule your meetings, because you are more alert.

3. It's Okay to Say NO!

You make a lot of decisions between the time you wake up and when you go to sleep every day. You face an enormous amount of choices and options at any given point in time, and your choice can either perpetuate the chaos in your life or end it. You commit each time you say yes to something or someone. What you might not realise is that every time you accept something, you deny yourself an opportunity to do something else.

For your peace of mind, learn to say no. Each time you agree to something, you make a conscious choice to commit your time and energy. You can easily free up these resources and commit them to something better, more productive, by saying no. The lesson here is that you should try and avoid being too available to everyone and everything.

4. Plan Your Life

While chaos is usually disruptive, you can restore calm and order by planning your days. Planning gives you purpose and a guideline for pursuing your goals. There's so much to achieve in life, and you can do that through planning. When things are difficult, planning can change your perspective and approach to life. It helps you focus and bring intention into your activities. Planning gives you a new perspective on what you need to do and how best to go about it.

Personal Improvement Goals

An interesting thing about the human conscience is that more often, everyone is aware of their flaws. The only difference is that while some people might live in denial about them, others choose to do something about it and improve their lives. To make such personal improvements, you must first recognise your flaws, realise the negative impact they have on your life, and from there, come up with a strategy to become a better person. All this means you need to focus. Since everyone has unique personal improvement goals, let's discuss some of the most common ones, and through it, you'll learn how to work around yours.

1. Finding Your Purpose in Life

It's interesting when you think about it. Most people say they know their purpose in life, but if you prod further, you realise they don't. Without knowing your purpose, you might struggle to get any sense of direction in life. Listen to your gut, identify your strengths and weaknesses, think of the things that inspire you, note down some of your achievements and successes. These are some simple actions that can help you realise your purpose in life.

Finding out your purpose is one thing; what to do with it is an even bigger challenge. Luckily, life is one big school with lessons at every turn. Nurture these skills, abilities, and passions. After identifying your strengths, for example, enrol in a course to improve them. Build on your successes and achievements. Your purpose in life doesn't necessarily have to be landing on Mars, but if it is, why not go for it? What's stopping you?

2. Improving Personal Relationships

Personal relationships are important in many ways. Their impact on your life influences your personality. Families and other social constructs can be complicated. One thing that many people have in common is that there is always a relationship they need to improve or fix, even when it seems like everything is going right. Even the best relationships still need work from time to time.

As we evolve, so do our relationships. Relationships also carry a lot of feelings and emotions, most of which are often unsaid. We tend to take a lot of relationships for granted. To improve any relationship, you must first evaluate it and understand its imbalance. From there, determine what aspects of the relationship need work. For example, you might have a good working relationship with your colleagues, but your communication skills need some work. Talk to them about it and have everyone express their concerns.

Personal relationships consume so much of your

energy, so make sure that energy is well spent. Strained relationships can have quite a ripple effect that might distract you from focusing on what really matters—your personal goals.

3. Learn New Skills

In your career and personal life, new skills are always useful. Personal development involves either learning new skills, sharpening the ones you have, and at times dropping some bad habits. Most skills are acquired, and you can improve them through practice. This is perhaps one of the personal improvement objectives that will stay with you throughout your lifetime. Go on and take a class, find a mentor, go for counselling, there's so much to learn that can help you improve your life.

4. Develop a Higher Level of Self-Esteem

Lack of confidence and low self-esteem are some of the common reasons why most people are stuck in boring, unfulfilling lives, friendships, relationships, and careers. You know you can and want to do more, but you somehow lack that impetus to step up and take the challenge. What's more interesting about this is how self-esteem and confidence are tied to the first three personal improvement goals. In retrospect, this should be the first thing you work on.

Self-esteem makes you feel good about your life. It

helps you eliminate self-doubt and embrace the level of confidence that will yield success. For most people, it is easier said than done, and this is what robs them of many opportunities that come their way.

You compare yourself to other people's achievements without realizing that each of you is running a different race. Each time you focus on things that are not working in your life, you fail to appreciate every other thing that's going on well. In the long run, you are caught up in the unending cycle of worrying about things that you cannot change. It feels terrible when you try and fail, and this negative energy can be overwhelming.

One of the greatest aspects of personal development is to make peace with the fact that you cannot change everything. Spend more energy on things that you are good at. Identify your strengths, develop them, and try to achieve more success with them. That success can bring you confidence and a platform to improve your weaknesses, too.

Celebrate your wins regardless of the size, and more importantly, remember that your circumstances do not define you. Every new day is a chance to do better and become an amazing person. Above everything else, to succeed in living the life you want you have to focus on yourself. The world has changed, and people are more preoccupied with their lives than what's going on in yours. Just do you!

Walking the Talk

In the previous section, we talked about common personal development goals whose pursuit can improve your life. We now take the next step and put those ideas into action. Goals are useless if you can't act on them. It's important to work on your goals because their accomplishment gets you closer to wholesome success in both your personal and professional life.

Earlier on we talked about having a clear sense of direction and purpose in life. All this is possible when you have clearly outlined goals. It is easier to accomplish tasks when you know what you are doing and why. In the process, you learn to prioritise tasks and events on your schedule, time allocation and the need for delegation. All this culminates into learning how to identify and eliminate distractions from your life because you understand the value of your input.

Your commitment to realising your personal goals can also improve your work ethic because of your dedication to the cause. Having a clear vision can spur your motivation, giving you renewed energy on everything you are working on. You already know what you are focusing on, so let's look at simple steps to get you there:

1. Define your Vision

Assess your desires, ambition and performance to ensure that they align with your self-improvement goals. Based on these goals, you can create a vision for where you want to be in a few years, what you should achieve to consider your plans a success, and more importantly, the timeline for achieving these goals. Follow the same principles of setting strategic goals to define your vision. Thus, your vision should be specific, measurable, actionable, realistic and time-conscious (SMART) (O'Neill et al., 2006).

2. Plan of Action

Having defined your vision, you need an action plan to bring it to life. Think of how to improve different aspects of your life, so that you can realise your set objectives. What can you do to improve in each of them?

When developing an action plan, you might realise that some goals are bigger than others, or require considerably more effort. In such cases, the best thing to do is to break them down into smaller, manageable milestones. Even as you work on your plans, don't forget that one of the most important aspects of self-improvement is learning. Your willingness to learn is directly proportional to how much improvement you can actualise through your plans.

3. Monitor Progress

Once your plans are in motion, you need a means of measuring progress. How can you tell whether you are heading in the right direction? How do you know if you are making progress or not? Come up with a means of measuring progress, and through it, identify all the changes that take place and the impact they have on your life. With time, it becomes easier to identify the practices that get you closer to your goals and those that hold you back.

4. Evaluation and Improvement

If you've made it this far, it is safe to say that you have everything in place. Your vision for the future is clear, your plans are in motion, and you have measures in place to monitor progress. Remember when we mentioned that there is a lot of learning involved? Well, this is where it all comes together.

As you monitor progress, you must also identify where you fall short. Review your processes and find out where you can make improvements. Regular reviews can help you identify whether your cause is still worth the time and resources you've committed to it. Up to the most recent progress report, what have you learned about yourself? Are you still on course to achieve your goals within the set timelines? Do you need to make adjustments? Have your goals changed? The purpose of an evaluation is to get a reality check of all the progress made so far and either build on it or rethink your goals, strategies and approaches.

Ultimately, the kind of life you want to live is within your reach. You just need to reach for it and never let go. You learn a lot on your journey to self-improvement that can help you think clearly and focus on the things that matter. You gain insight into your interactions and learn how to build better relationships and connections in the process. Personal development can also make you more productive by establishing structure in your life.

CHAPTER FOUR

Confidence

Confidence is a term you come across all the time. You use it so often in conversations, you probably have never stopped to think about what it means. Do you ever feel like people around you are bolder, surer of themselves and everything they do, than you are? This is a common feeling that many people experience. When this happens, you doubt your skills and abilities and worry that perhaps, you might never be as good or as bold as they are. What you might not realise, is that the people you look up to might also share similar concerns. How is it possible, therefore, that they can harbour similar concerns, yet still appear so bold they'd make the best power brokers ever? It's simple—confidence! They might not have it all the time, but they certainly know how to create it when it matters.

Confidence speaks to your belief in yourself, your skills, and your abilities. It is that personal conviction that you are good enough, and have what it takes to tackle all the challenges life throws at you. It is the driving force behind the triumphs of many successful people, and more importantly, an honest and realistic assessment of your abilities, and security in the knowledge thereof. Perfection is an illusion. Chasing perfection will only ever yield disappointment. However, by understanding your strengths and weaknesses, you feel secure because you know your limits.

The thing about confidence is that it gives you that certainty that you can do whatever you put your mind to. It is an innate belief that you call upon from time to time. Granted, we all don't have the same level of confidence, but you can learn and improve gradually. Before we jump into the gist of confidence, we must point out that confidence might not be the answer to all your problems. Bad days, mishaps, and disappointments happen to everyone all the time, regardless of how confident you are. It also doesn't mean that you will be certain about yourself all the time. More importantly, confidence isn't an inference that you know everything and can do anything you want. It is, however, trusting that whatever happens in whichever circumstance, you can face it and learn from it.

So, why is confidence so important?

Confidence is a good thing because when you tap into it, you can make the best first impression ever. You handle difficult or stressful situations better, speak with authority and conviction, and the best of all, make it easier for people to trust and be easy around you.

Every aspect of your life benefits from a hint of confidence from time to time. In most cases, you won't need it. However, when you need it the most, you better have it. Life throws a lot at you every single day. Many are the times when you feel drained, ready to throw in the towel and accept defeat. It's during such moments when giving up feels like the only option when confidence makes a difference. All it takes is a fraction of a second to alter the course of your destiny.

The need for confidence might also come with your reputation or obligation. For example, if you are in a position of leadership, confidence is almost non-negotiable. People look up to you as their leader. To inspire them, they need to trust you. When you put together a team for whatever reason, you must first be sure of yourself. Without confidence, you cannot guide that team. They will lose interest, and since you cannot convince them otherwise, you might as well forget about realizing your shared goals. It gets even worse if someone else in the team is bolder, more confident than you are—you become a subordinate.

Away from leadership roles and the workplace, confidence will also help you forge strategic relationships that can help you thrive in different capacities. Even in your relationships, you have to be bold enough to attract the kind of partner you want. You should be confident that you are good enough, and worthy of a healthy, fulfilling relationship. Your willingness to pursue new opportunities is necessary for personal growth.

In essence, confidence is a state of mind; your mood at a particular time. Confidence is about what and how you feel about yourself at a given time. Remember when we talked about how people around you usually seem to be bolder and more sure of themselves, yet they probably share the same worries and concerns as you do? This is how they do it. Regardless of what you are going through, or what is going on around you, you can always change your state of mind.

Confidence generally revolves around the following aspects:

1. Positive Mindset

You waste a lot of time worrying about all the ways things might fail. Instead, change your mentality and focus on the present. Focus on doing the right thing right now. Note that your reality derives from what you train your mind on. Changing your mindset can easily alter your mental state.

2. Body Language

Your body language speaks louder than your words. If you want to be more confident, you must learn the psychology of body language and how to tap into it successfully. Think of anyone you consider one of the most confident people you know. What's their demeanour when talking about something? How do they carry themselves?

A firm handshake, maintaining eye contact, and sitting straight are simple things we take for granted, yet when it matters most, they make a big difference. The way you present yourself to an audience speaks volumes and can give the impression of confidence, even when you are full of doubt.

3. Growth Mindset

Life is a school with lessons at every turn. Confidence is not limited to the triumphs of your effort. You can learn so much from a position of failure, enough to build your confidence. Confidence comes from within, not from the achievements or failures, but from the lessons you internalise from them. A growth mindset means that you are willing to learn. Instead of giving up, you come back stronger and with a different perspective; you try again.

Taking Stock of the Missed Opportunities

Many people suffer from a lack of confidence. Even with all the education, talent, and experience they have, their performance and success are undermined by a lack of confidence and limiting beliefs. Such beliefs make you doubt your abilities and think you will never be good enough. This is how big opportunities pass you by.

Frankly, lack of confidence is not a mistake. More often, it is the result of a negative mindset perpetuated by persistent feelings of worthlessness and inadequacy. It might also be a result of social problems—like bad experiences at home or anywhere else in your community—stress, anxiety, and depression.

Persistent negativity can cause adverse effects on your life, especially in the way you think about yourself. It eventually has a degrading influence on your actions, behaviour, thoughts, and experiences in life. Given all the challenges in life, most people end up focusing more on achievements, without paying attention to the stressors or reasons why they constantly doubt their skills and abilities. This is how lack of confidence robs you of the opportunity to live a fulfilling life. Below are common effects you might experience:

1. Aversion to Criticism

Criticism is important for growth. Whether in your personal or professional career, you will not always see things the same way as everyone else. People will always have contrary opinions, ideas, processes to yours, and that's okay. Lack of confidence creates an aversion to criticism such that you believe your way should be the only way.

People who struggle with this feel like criticism is a personal attack. If someone has a contrary opinion, they feel you are coming after them and take it personally.

They might even feel you think they don't belong there. This happens because of the constant negative thoughts they've wrapped themselves in. Eventually, their productivity wanes just as their motivation did, and any form of criticism leads to conflict.

2. Indecision

Indecision is one of the reasons why people lose out on great opportunities. This happens because of false positives in your mind. Even when it's a decision about something simple, you still find it difficult to make a straight decision. There are many times in life when the difference between success and failure is a moment of quick thinking. If you are unable to process things fast, you can miss out on so much.

3. Risk Avoidance

A common consequence of low confidence is risk avoidance. You always try to play things safe, and when you have to choose something, you always go for the least adventurous. In your professional life, for example, you turn down opportunities to advance your career because you are comfortable with what you have. Leadership roles come and go, but you don't take them because you are unsure of what lies ahead. You worry about what people might think of you if you fail at that role. Usually, you are more afraid of people finding out you might not be up to the task than the failure itself. For this reason, you avoid opportunities that cast you in the spotlight.

4. Low Self-Worth

We all go through moments when we are displeased with who we are or what we do. However, people who struggle with low confidence take it a notch higher, and it becomes self-hatred. It gets so bad, you can't forgive yourself even for the simplest mistakes.

The problem with this is that you feel worthless and that feeling becomes deep-rooted in your life. It makes you feel you don't deserve the opportunities that come your way, or that you are not as valuable as others around you. Self-worth is not given to anyone, you build it by being confident in your abilities.

5. Unhealthy Relationships

When you harbour negative perceptions about yourself, you usually feel like everyone feels the same way too. Your relationships, both personal and professional, are not fulfilling because you never present your true self. When you meet people, you try to cultivate a personality that seems likeable or acceptable so that you can fit in. You might even do things that you are uncomfortable with, or you don't believe in so that people don't realise your weakness—the negative way you see yourself.

The problem with this is that your social life becomes a lie. You maintain different personalities to fit in with everyone according to what you think their rules are. You might pull this off successfully, but deep down, your situation only gets worse. Your social and professional relationships don't represent what you believe in.

6. Imperfect Perfection

The pursuit of perfection is one of the most devastating effects of lack of confidence. Such perfectionists believe that they will never be good enough, even after a series of accomplishments. They don't even trust people who see and praise their achievements because their lives revolve around a constant perception of failure.

As you can see above, a lack of confidence can ruin your life. It can bring problems in your professional and private life. People feel insecure for many different reasons. This, however, does not define who you are. It is important to try and understand the underlying reason why you feel inadequate and address it. This is probably the most honest conversation you will ever have with yourself. It is only until you address and remove those causes that you will be able to restore your life to the path of success.

Building Self-Confidence

One of the greatest strengths of the human species is the ability to experience a range of emotions depending on different stimuli in your environment. At the same time, we are also able to control how we respond to emotions. How confident you feel about a situation or someone usually depends on the emotions evoked from that interaction. Building self-confidence means being in control so that your emotions don't dictate your experiences.

It's always wise to try and understand why you feel what you do, what triggers your emotions, and so on. This is important because your behaviour, thoughts, and actions depend on how you feel. Whether you feel confident or not, you are always in charge of your feelings. No one can tell you how to feel and make you do it. Confidence builds the moment you understand that you have full control over your feelings.

Confidence and Purpose

Confidence building is about certainty, the belief that you can accomplish what you put your mind to. Confidence also comes with a sense of purpose and direction. Think about it for a moment, why is it important to you that you learn how to build your confidence? Are you preparing for a presentation in front of a huge gathering? Are you trying to get the attention of your crush and take that first step? Do you need to make a good impression on an investor to get that contract you've been chasing for months? To build your confidence, you must first understand why and what you want to achieve.

Once you realise your purpose, all you have to do is train your brain to unlearn the defeating concepts and replace them with healthier alternatives. Even if you are not confident, it helps to portray yourself as a confident person. That demeanour alone can open many doors for you. Try to ignore all the uncertainty and doubt, because they will only hold you back. As the negative thoughts fizzle away, you feel more confident standing up for yourself. Without the negative sentiments, your body and brain learn to create a positive feedback loop.

A Different Outlook

For most people, confidence building involves rethinking their core beliefs and eliminating those that have spurred self-doubt. What questions come to mind whenever you are faced with a difficult situation? If they are all negative, for example, '*Do they see me as a failure?*' then you need to change your perspective. Try to shift your perspective from that negativity to more positive thoughts. For example, '*Why not? What's stopping me from doing it?*'

At times the secret lies in how you frame the questions in your mind. If you walk into any situation conscious that you can handle it, then, whatever happens, you will handle it. In the worst scenario, you will at least make an attempt. This is why a change of perspective is important.

A positive outlook will help you improve your skills and become more receptive to new knowledge and information. Challenges and obstacles are nothing but opportunities to learn a new concept. This gives you more assurance than avoiding them altogether. With time, you will rethink most setbacks you've had in life and see the underlying opportunities in them. That is how you build confidence.

Positivity

Another powerful confidence builder is positivity. While negative thoughts degrade your life, positive thoughts are empowering. You have a higher chance of accomplishing something when you believe you believe you can do it. You approach it with determination. On the other hand, if you don't believe you can do it, you approach it half-heartedly and give up at the earliest sign of difficulty.

Positivity thrives on self-knowledge. What are your strengths and weaknesses? What lessons can you learn from them? It might sound easier on paper because most of the time, we channel our energy towards things that we are unhappy about. The most you can achieve is magnifying them into bigger issues than they were supposed to be. This is how negative thoughts kill your confidence.

A better way out of this is to recondition your thought process. Fully aware of your strengths and weaknesses, discuss them with people who care about your progress, for example, supportive family members and friends. If possible, ask them to add more points to your list of strengths and weaknesses. From there, find out how you can manage, or at least improve, your weaknesses. Be bolder; celebrate and appreciate your strengths.

People make mistakes all the time. Use them as learning opportunities instead of seeing them as negatives. Praise yourself when you do something good, and accept compliments from others. Appreciate it, and politely ask them what they liked about your input, what they think you can improve to make it even better. This will be great for your confidence. Celebrate your wins with friends and family members too.

Criticism, though often misused by malicious people who know about your confidence struggles, is one of the best learning experiences you have. People see things differently, and you will not always agree on everything. Whether you accept the criticism or not, you have to be assertive. Listen to what people say and decide what to do about their opinions later. Responding defensively will only give them a chance to retort and from there, things can go south so fast.

Take a Leap of Faith

It takes some practice to be good at something. Remember the first time you rode a bike or drove a car? It wasn't easy. However, you kept going at it until you mastered the skills. Today you can drive for hours on end, manoeuvre through insane traffic, and push your limits on the freeway.

The lesson here is that your confidence grows with each task or goal you accomplish. You can drive the car through the rain, react fast to avoid an accident, and many other skills that make you a good driver.

When you started driving, none of this was achievable. It almost seemed impossible to accomplish, and you can remember the number of times you froze when a huge truck was driving ahead of you. You were probably too afraid to overtake.

The difference between your driving skills as a learner and today is experience. Your confidence grows the longer you try something and familiarise yourself with the conditions. Note, however, you must take the leap of faith. From a point of low confidence, taking that first step might not be easy. Starting something for the first time can be difficult, and for this, your willingness to learn, a positive mindset, and adequate preparation will make a big difference.

Whatever you must do for confidence building, always believe that you are good enough, and give it your best shot. Having seen the relationship between confidence and emotions, it's safe to say the only thing holding you back from being confident is your mind. Stop living in your own head. The limiting beliefs that hold you back only exist in your mind. The beliefs that constantly remind you that you are not worthy are not real. They are but a figment of your imagination. You are strong enough to bounce back from adversity. Stop holding onto the weights that pull you down.

Overcoming Confidence Killers

In your pursuit of success, you will come across a lot of confidence killers out there. Success doesn't come easy, and most of the obstacles you encounter could knock you down and have you rethink your approach altogether. The thing about external obstacles is that in most cases, you can't control them, and can only react or respond to their attempts at holding you back.

Now, there's another set of obstacles that you can control: those that live within. While it is generally easy to identify the external obstacles, the enemies within can cause even more harm and damage to your confidence. This is because they drain your purpose and potential, demotivate you, and fill your life with regret.

You see, the biggest challenge with internal confidence killers is that it is impossible to fight an enemy you can't see, one that you don't even know exists, and that thrives off the same resources you need to succeed. If you don't figure them out and find a way around them, your plans will never materialise. Below are some of the silent obstacles that are killing your confidence:

1. Overthinking

This is one of the greatest enemies of progress. Overthinkers live on the edge, and not the thrilling or exciting kind. Nothing seems easy to you. In your mind, there's always a nasty surprise lurking in the background.

You don't believe that people can do good things out of pure intentions, and are always worrying about the worst things happening. You drown in constant worry and make things look worse than they are.

Overthinkers also tend to dramatise things. You script everything in your mind and believe that life will unravel the way you played it out in your mind. None of this is real, and the danger you worry about is but a figment of your imagination. Believe it or not, you have the power to undo the script and let that narrative go. Your story doesn't have to end that way.

Stop for a moment and let life unfold before your eyes. The thing about overthinking is that it is usually a manifestation of something you are deeply concerned about. Dig deeper and trace the moment these thoughts started, and from there, you can claw your way back and rebuild your confidence.

2. Undervaluing Yourself

Personal undervaluation is a common limiting factor that kills your confidence. When you feel unworthy, nothing that people say about you will ever make you feel any different. Your judgment is so clouded that you can't see how good you are. Self-confidence is a product of embracing who you are and your accomplishments. It is about self-belief and being your biggest cheerleader. By doubting yourself, you are essentially devaluing your life.

There are many possible reasons why you might feel unworthy. It could be anything from childhood upbringing to traumatic events in your adult life. Whichever the case, it is never too late to learn how to love and appreciate yourself more.

3. Negative Environment

The person you are today is the product of everything in your immediate environment. If you surround yourself with negativity, your life will be filled with negative energy. Check your company, for they could be the reason why your confidence is always low. Being around negative people is worse than being alone. Be it your friends or family members, if the relationship is hurting your confidence, it will never do you any good, no matter how many times you wish they could change. For your peace of mind and the sake of your prosperity, walk away.

4. Thinking You Don't Deserve Good Things

The most painful reality many people have come to realise, usually at a great expense, is that the grass isn't always greener on the other side. If you water and tend to yours, it will be just as green, if not better. What you might not realise is that while you think good things only happen to other people, other people wish they had the life you have.

Regardless of what they tell you or what you see, you will never truly know what goes on in people's lives. That grass you think is greener than yours, you don't know what it takes to keep it that way. Maybe it's a smokescreen—it usually is! Be grateful for your life and everything you have, and for those that you don't have, be patient, and keep working. Your luck will eventually turn.

5. Living in Your Past

The most you can do with your past is learn from it. Everyone has some actions, experiences, and decisions that they wish they could undo or do differently if they had a second chance. It could be anything from a missed opportunity to someone you took for granted, but all that is gone. It is called the past for a reason; it is gone, and you can't change it. You can take the lessons from it, however, and use them to make your present better as you work on a promising future.

Don't allow past events to hold you hostage and kill your confidence. So what if you failed last time? That doesn't mean you give up altogether. If anything, use the failed attempts to bounce back even harder. People fail all the time. Even the greatest men and women alive have failed more times than they have succeeded. Yet, the glory of a single success is remembered throughout history.

England 0 - 0 Uruguay 1966, Spain 0 - 1 Switzerland 2010. These were disappointing opening group stage results at their respective FIFA World Cup events, not to mention Italy in 1982, who drew all their games in the group stage against Poland, Cameroon, and Peru, and only sneaked into the next round because of a superior goal difference to Peru and Cameroon.

Not many people remember these results. However, they remember that England, Italy and Spain were crowned World Cup champions in 1966, 1982, and 2010 respectively. Failure doesn't mean you will never succeed. The lesson here is that a bad start doesn't mean your race is run.

Focus on what you have, not what you lack. Practice gratitude; it goes a long way in making you confident with what you have. Remember that someone will always be worse off than you are, no matter how bad things are going for you. Even if things are looking up, someone else will always have it much better. Gratitude helps you appreciate everything you have, your skills, abilities, strengths, weaknesses, you name it. If you ever feel short of confidence, look back at everything you have achieved, and remember how much you prayed for them, and how hard you worked to come this far.

CHAPTER FIVE

Controlling Emotions

James is the operations manager in a fast-growing freight forwarding firm.

Angela is pursuing her passion for art, and recently opened an art gallery downtown, which, to her surprise, has been a success.

Stella is in her third year working as a student nurse in a local community college.

Each of the individuals mentioned above is living a unique life, and they live worlds apart from one another. Their paths might never even cross. However, underneath the surface, they share similarities that make them closer than you know.

You see, James is going through a difficult divorce, and going by proceedings, it doesn't look like the outcome will favour him. He lost custody of the kids, and they like their mom's new place more than his. The unfolding events have distracted him for a long time, and as a result, he's barely the same person he was when he got promoted to operations manager. His co-workers have perfected the art of reading his moods and steering clear when he's not in the best shape.

Angela's new art gallery might be thriving, but she is frustrated and can barely hide it every time she receives a call or an email from a former business partner who is suing her for damages over breach of contract.

After three years in the institution, Stella cares deeply for the students under her care. She's been like a guardian to most of them, and together with different student organizations, she's championed a lot of awareness projects that have transformed the health culture in the institution. However, she recently learned that due to budget cuts, her department will be wound up. The college favours a new arrangement with the local hospitals instead of operating their unit. Stella is anxious because she doesn't know what the future holds for her students.

James, Angela, and Stella are strangers in different parts of the world, yet they are drawn together by one thing: the fact that their productivity and effectiveness at work is threatened by their emotions. Indeed, they still go about their duties with a semblance of normalcy, but this is merely a facade. There's an aspect of emotional self-control missing in their lives, and however much they try to put up a good fight, things will never be the same again.

Emotional self-control refers to your ability to **manage** uncomfortable emotions, especially in difficult situations, without affecting your productivity. We must highlight the use of the word *manage*. One of the biggest challenges many people have today is that they **suppress** their emotions. Suppression is simply avoidance or denial, and is an ineffective way of addressing your emotions. More often, suppression yields more problems than solutions.

Management means allowing yourself to experience both positive and negative emotions. Wouldn't life be awesome if it was all positive vibes and good times? The harsh reality is that negative emotions are a part of life. They can build your character, and that is what makes life so rich and fulfilling. Managing emotions means that instead of suppressing the negative emotions, you allow yourself to process and understand them within the appropriate context. Emotional self-control is the key to staying calm and level-headed in any situation, professional or personal. This is also how you can easily avoid unnecessary conflicts.

Let's briefly explain the science behind emotional self-control:

The prefrontal cortex and amygdala are parts of the brain that play a key role in emotional regulation. The prefrontal cortex is the part of the brain tasked with planning, expressing your personality traits, your social behaviour, and decision making. The amygdala is the part of your brain that decodes emotion, especially anything that poses a threat to you. From this explanation, the amygdala processes your body's alarm responses whenever you are threatened. It is through the amygdala, therefore, that your brain processes conditioned fear.

The human brain is wired for survival. To this end, the amygdala's function takes precedence when it detects a threat, overriding all the other functions of your brain, and in particular, the prefrontal cortex. This process is known as the amygdala hijack.

When an amygdala hijack is in play, the brain focuses on the perceived threat, and how to overcome it. Assuming that you are in the office when this hijack takes place, your attention shifts from the task you were working on to the threat, or whatever it is that has unsettled you. At this point, your brain prioritises any information relevant to the threat over everything else.

More often, the amygdala makes mistakes in such situations because it only receives a partial picture of the threat, but has to act on it instantly. This also happens because the amygdala doesn't receive all the information relayed to your sensory organs. The parts of your brain that collect information from sensory organs analyse them better and more accurately, but it takes longer. This is why the amygdala only receives a fraction of the information and is prone to mistakes. As a result, the amygdala will react to perceived threats as though they were actual threats, and this is why you overreact to a situation, and probably regret it later.

Emotions and Decision Making

How did you go about the most recent big decision in your life? Did you weigh the advantages and disadvantages or go with your gut feeling? Granted, many people listen to their gut because their choice represents their truest desires. However, after a closer look, you will realise that there's always an emotional aspect in play even when you think your decisions are a result of common sense and logic. Ideally, you need to strike a balance between your gut feeling and reason. To make the right decision, you have to understand the relationship between your thought process and emotions.

Emotions arise from the brain's interpretation of things happening around you, based on your beliefs, thoughts, and memories. This informs your behaviour and feelings. In a way, all decisions you make are a function of this process.

Let's say you were chased down the street by a dog on your way to work in the morning. There's a high chance you will not use that street in the afternoon. You'll probably take a bus home, because walking down that street evokes fear. This action will override the fact that you usually enjoy walking home, or the weather is just perfect. Without the incident with the dog, you are always happy to walk home. Even though there might be some logic in either of these decisions, your reaction after the incident is a result of your emotional state.

Each emotion influences your decisions differently. For example, exhaustion, fear, or unhappiness can make you accept uncomfortable conditions or circumstances, like staying in a bad relationship or ignoring the opportunity to apply for a promotion. Other than the kind of decision you make, emotions can also influence the speed with which you make a decision. Impatient, rash decisions are common when you are angry, because you probably want to get something done and out of your mind. The same is possible when you are exhilarated. You ride the pleasant high without thinking of the consequences.

What we realise, therefore, is that intuition will always play a role in your decisions, whether you rationalise or not. While it is okay to listen to your gut, you must also be careful to avoid responding based on an unconscious bias, poor judgement, risk aversion, or carelessness.

Since logic and emotions both influence your decisions, you need to understand the background of your emotions, and from there, how that foundation affects your behaviour and thought process. This makes it easier to not only manage your responses, but also make better choices. That being said, emotions can have a positive impact on your decisions in the following ways:

1. Out of decency, you can choose compassion and respect for another person.

2. Emotions can help you understand the context of a situation, hence a faster and more impactful decision.

3. Emotions make you decide faster than rationalising a situation. This is usually a reactive response and can be useful in the face of danger.

4. By considering the emotional impact of your decisions, you care about their outcome and the impact the decisions will have on those around you.

5. When facing almost similar options, some logical decisions might require an emotional impact to determine the best outcome.

You must also exercise caution with emotional decision-making because it can yield the following challenges:

1. Most emotional decisions are irrational. You respond without understanding the magnitude of the situation. Thus, you act on a whim and then go to great lengths trying to justify a bad decision.

2. You might project your emotions onto someone, but there's no guarantee that their

interpretation will fit your expected outcome. This is how some misunderstandings arise.

3. Intense emotions can override rational thought, especially in instances where rationality was necessary.

From the positive and negative influences discussed, we realise that ideal solutions should consider both emotional and rational aspects of your being. No better mood puts you in the best frame of mind to decide, because every mood influences your decisions in some way. Therefore, an ideal solution is to recognise the fact that emotions will always be in play when making decisions; understand and try to prevent them from overriding your rational thought process. You can get the best of both worlds in the following ways:

1. Consider Important Factors

Before making a decision, consider all the factors. List down all the positives and negatives, then assign values to them which you will use to prioritise their role in your decision. Note, however, that in some cases, unrelated emotions might also influence your decision.

Some factors, like the weather, can also influence your emotional state, even though they are not related to the issue at hand. Be certain your decision is not influenced by the gloomy weather or terrible news.

2. Insight into Your Emotions

Most of the time, emotions alert you to something you should pay attention to before making a decision. Recognise your emotional state before making a decision and then think about the logic behind it. For example, if you feel angry, your brain might be telling you something's not right. Perhaps you are a victim of abuse, and you need to do something about it. Listen to this anger, but instead of being abrasive, find a better way to assert your decision.

If you are overly excited about something, maybe buying a house or a car, don't sign a contract just yet. Take time and evaluate the reason for your excitement. What is it about the car or the house that's suddenly got you over the moon? Sales representatives are keen on such moments and could take advantage of you. The last thing you want is to make such a commitment without due diligence. Many people have made such a mistake, only to realise later that their emotional state clouded their judgment, and they missed a better alternative.

3. Delay the Response

Don't be in a rush to make a decision. It might be difficult, especially if you feel you have the perfect response. However, an emotionally-charged response will almost always end in a disaster. If the event, person, or situation triggered your emotions, don't be in a hurry to give a response. Think it through and respond later with a clear mind.

Even though emotions play an important role in decision making, your resolve should not be based purely on your emotional state. Trust your gut, but don't do it blindly. Look for tangible proof to validate your gut feeling, and data and facts to assert your position. That being said, your gut feelings send signals from your prefrontal cortex, so you should never dismiss them entirely.

Understanding Emotional Conflict

You meet different people every day: customers, colleagues, friends, family members, and strangers. Each of these interactions involves some emotional response. We all have different views and opinions, and for that reason, disagreement and arguments are common. Conflict arises when at least two parties have different opinions on something. Similarly, an emotional conflict is an intrapersonal situation where you experience more than one emotion, and cannot easily identify which of the emotions is ideal for your present situation.

Let's take an example of a common situation at work. Going about your duties, you constantly make decisions that go against your core values and personal beliefs, but on the other hand, are profitable for the business. In such situations, you are torn between the happiness you experience from success and the guilt of going against your personal values.

The same can happen in your social circles too. Perhaps when you get together with your friends and family members, you engage in some activities or some conversations that don't align with your personal views, but since you don't want to go against the grain or be the black sheep in the family, you go with the flow.

Such instances of emotional conflict have taken a toll on many people before, to a point where you become disillusioned with life in general. Constantly overriding your core values and beliefs for the greater good is a level of compromise that slowly erodes the foundation of your being. At some point, you might start wondering whether anything is worthwhile anymore.

Emotions can run high in any encounter because everyone believes their way is the right way. For your well-being, it is important to learn how to manage conflicting emotions. Before you do, however, let's look at some reasons why such conflicts arise frequently:

1. Rigid Rules and Policies

The rigidity of rules and policies is a common reason why emotional conflicts arise, and this is true even for unwritten rules in social interactions. You seek growth in your professional and personal life. However, growth will only come when you embrace change. Unfortunately, the nature of some rules and policies do not reflect this evolutionary concept.

This explains why you feel emotionally drained when interacting with some friends or family members. Your interactions, and the core structure of your relationships, are defined by long-standing norms, written or otherwise, yet they don't recognise the fact that your life has transformed over the years, and you might not share the same views anymore.

2. Miscommunication

Communication, or lack thereof, is a common reason for emotional conflict. Without proper communication about important issues there's bound to be a misunderstanding, whether at work or in your relationships. In a professional circle, communication is usually direct, especially when giving instructions. Things get a bit complicated in personal relationships because you must also consider non-verbal gestures.

3. Unmet Expectations

Have you ever been in a situation where your role or purpose feels vaguer than you are led to believe? In professional circles, this happens when you feel underutilised, and the growth opportunities that you might have been promised don't seem to be forthcoming. You have so much hope for the future, and trusting in your abilities, believe that you've got so much to offer. However, since the establishment isn't aligned with your expectations, you are torn between staying the course to keep your job, or walking away to find a better opportunity. The problem with such instances is that the longer you stay put, the more demotivated you are, and your work becomes less enjoyable over time.

Unmet expectations are not isolated to your professional life and are a common point of conflict in many relationships. Eventually, it comes down to staying together but lowering your expectations of your partner, especially when you realise that they will never change, or moving on to a relationship where your needs and expectations are met.

If any of the issues raised above are unsolved, you feel restricted, and might start thinking you are in the wrong place. That's the point you start searching for another job because you no longer feel appreciated in your current place of work. In your personal life, you start considering your options. You wonder whether being in that relationship is the right thing.

It is in your best interest, and that of everyone involved, to resolve the emotional conflict if you are to realise any progress in life. Even without conflict, decisions borne of emotional influence don't usually turn out to be the best ones. Now imagine a situation where your decisions are influenced by conflicting emotions. This is a recipe for disaster.

Managing Your Emotions

Everyone deserves to be in an environment that allows them to express and experience their emotions. Unfortunately, this does not usually happen. In our previous discussions, we have realised the important role that emotions play in your responses and reactions. It is therefore important that you get in sync with your emotions, and understand why they arise. This will go a long way in your decision making, day-to-day interactions, self-care, and successful relationships.

We generally worry more about uncomfortable emotions, yet every other emotion, including the positive ones like joy and elation, can become so intense that you are unable to control them, leaving you exposed.

In response to overwhelming emotions, everyone has a different coping mechanism, most of which are not usually effective or sustainable. Gaming, binge-watching TV, and excessive drinking are some common unhealthy strategies people use. Another counter-productive approach that many people use to manage uncomfortable emotions is to ignore them, hoping they will pass. In each of these instances, you can only push the emotions away for so long. Eventually, they erupt, and usually when you least expect it, and in the worst possible circumstances. It gets worse; continuous emotional suppression is often linked to several psychological and health problems.

The thing about managing emotions is that you will not always have the luxury of time to perhaps think about them, maybe consider the context or the environment, and so on. More often, you have to work your way on the go, especially in the corporate sector. It is only until you get home in the evening, or when you get some free time, that you can reflect on your day. So, how can you manage such emotions at the moment?

What can you do to respond diligently instead of reacting aggressively to an emotionally-charged situation? Let's look at some useful tips below:

1. Communicating Displeasure

Your preferred mode of communication can make a bad situation worse. In your workplace, most communication is official. However, if you need to share negative emotions with someone, do it over the phone, or in person. Sending an email or leaving them a message on their answering machine is too impersonal, and will probably make the situation worse. This also applies to personal relationships. Expressing yourself in person makes it easier for the recipient to understand the magnitude of their actions, and probably explain a misunderstanding.

2. Find Common Ground

You can diffuse a tense situation by compromising. Instead of a terse response, the phrase 'I *understand*' can help you tone down the tension, and agree with someone. At the same time, you should also pay attention to your feelings. Before you compromise, do you feel threatened by what someone is trying to tell you? If you are in such a position, try not to shut down, or defend yourself against the other person. This blocks them and any possibility of a compromise.

3. Make Polite Requests

If someone's actions are annoying, a polite request to do things differently is more useful than an angry outburst. Say an intern isn't doing something right. Instead of shouting at them, politely ask them to do it differently, or ask if they need help figuring it out because it looks like they're not doing it right. Apart from diffusing the emotional tension, you might even realise the intern was struggling, but out of fear didn't feel comfortable asking for help. You might have just made a breakthrough with the intern!

4. Take Responsibility

Instead of blaming people for your feelings, take responsibility for them and be open about it. When engulfed by emotion, you can easily blame someone without realizing it. For example, when you say '*You annoy me when you don't return my calls*', you shift the burden of your anger to the recipient. Instead, you can rephrase that statement as '*I feel so annoyed when you don't return my calls*'.

While the difference in the two statements might be subtle, the second one features an admission on your part. You own up to what you feel because you are responsible for it. You also inform the other person what their actions do to you.

5. Mediation

Before you act on conflicting emotions, assume the role of a mediator and consider both sides of the conflict. In the earlier example where you might be conflicted when spending time with friends, weigh your options. On one side, you understand that you've been friends for a long time and have been through so much together, and you don't want to break that bond. On the other hand, you are a different person now, grown, maybe with a family, and your personal views on the dynamics of your friendship have changed. So, how can you resolve this conflict without losing your friends, or compromising your identity? Have an honest discussion with your friends and express your concerns. You might not know it, but perhaps someone else shares the same concerns, but they haven't been bold enough to speak up. For example, you can't all be in your 30s, and still partying as you did in college, yet everyone is okay with it.

6. Maintain Decorum

Even though you might be frustrated or angry, don't be a child about it. Children throw a tantrum if something is not going their way. You are bigger and better than that. If you throw a fit each time you are annoyed, you create a toxic environment around you. People will start walking on eggshells whenever you are around, and might not express themselves freely for fear of what you might do next.

Your unpredictability makes you the last person anyone would want to collaborate with, and this might hinder your progress professionally or even at home. It's quite unfortunate when your partner, and maybe kids, feel more comfortable when you are away from home. A deathly silence ensues immediately when you get back.

Try and maintain your composure at work and home whenever you feel like things are not going according to plan. People make mistakes, and you should treat them as such, not an attack on your person. Create an enabling environment not just for your success, but also for people around you to thrive and grow with you.

Based on our discussions so far, it takes a lot of emotional processing to gain full control of your emotions. This level of access and understanding makes it easier for you to engage with other people in your professional and personal life. Ignored emotions can only worsen your interactions because they eventually surface in unfortunate incidents, like an angry outburst.

While it is always wise to talk about your emotions with someone and try to gain insight into them, you also have to be careful with whom, when, and what you share. There's a lot of emotional manipulation going on in the world today, so it's advisable to restrict such conversations with trusted members of your inner circle. This could include your mentor, supportive family members, and friends.

Many people express their emotions unreservedly so that they don't appear to be fake. While this authenticity is good, you must also realise the consequences that might arise from your interactions. This is where emotional discipline comes in. Try to understand your emotions and why they manifest in certain situations, or when you interact with specific people.

What do you feel about your present situation? Is your work fulfilling? Are you happy? Do you feel an emptiness in your life that you cannot understand? It's okay to reach out to a therapist or mentor to help you explore your concerns and understand them.

Mindfulness, meditation, and breathing exercises can help you manage your emotions during difficult times, especially if you are ever in a situation that triggers those emotions. You can also learn how to anticipate uncomfortable emotions and prepare an adequate response. If you are going to talk about your emotions with someone, plan your conversations strategically. Try to schedule difficult conversations at a time when the landing will be softer to cushion you against a blowback.

CHAPTER
SIX

Building Sustainable Success

What is your definition of success, and what does it mean to you? At what point do you look at achievements and realise you've made it? Most people have goals they work towards, each person's different from the other. Many goals are tangible, and since a lot of things in the world today revolve around money and numbers, our definition of success is usually underpinned by these factors. Life goals don't necessarily have to be limited to these metrics. It is okay to achieve them, but that's not all there is to success.

One thing we have to understand about success is that there are more ways to achieve it than most people are aware of. The highlight of success is to have a purpose and ensure it aligns with your goals. Life is not just about working towards something, it's also about understanding why you are committed to that cause.

In the past, a lot of people have come to a point in life where they feel that regardless of how successful they become, something is always missing. They lack that personal attachment to their success, that sense of fulfilment. If you are at that point, you need to rethink your idea of success. Likely, your measure of success has so far been limited to an arbitrary identifier, for example, net worth, income, bank account balance, or a title. None of these things matter if you don't find meaning in them.

There's a great disconnect between what we grow up learning about success and that sense of fulfilment you realise when you understand its true value. This explains why many people today seem to have it all, but are deeply disturbed by their inability to be truly happy. To feel confident about and appreciate your success, you must be able to define it, and why it is important to you.

The first step is to understand what your purpose is. Before you answer this question, take some time and reflect on your life. What do you want to achieve? Who do you want to become? On your deathbed, what must you have done that will make you trust that everything you achieved was worth it?

In the absence of purpose, you become a slave to someone else's goals. They realise their purpose through you. All the effort and resources you commit to every day helps them realise their purpose, but not yours. Power or financial success might conceal the emptiness, but will never fill the void in your life. Reflect on and identify your purpose. How are your current activities aligned to that purpose?

What impact do you have on the people around you? Being the social animals we are, a sense of community and belonging means so much. Like your purpose above, success without these connections might be difficult to sustain or measure. There's an element of satisfaction that comes from leaving a positive impact on other people's lives. The thing about personal success is that only a handful of people can, and have, been able to go it all alone.

Are you a better collaborator? Figuring out how your daily activities align with your purpose is one thing. However, if you can work on your goals and at the same time work alongside others with different talents, skills, and knowledge, you will realise both personal and professional growth in the same dimension. This is something we take for granted, but has always been an elusive feat for many people to achieve.

Success isn't just about your strengths and achievements. A huge part of it is about your weaknesses. Recognise them and be honest with yourself about them. Your weaknesses can bring you down if you can't handle them properly. Though a potential for your downfall, you can also work on them and turn them into huge opportunities.

If you are at a point in life where you think you've made it, how can you best describe that feeling? If you feel you haven't made it in life yet, how do you feel about it? What do you need to get there? Challenge the status quo and define your success on your terms.

What's Holding You Back?

We've all been at that plateau stage, where nothing seems to be working. You work hard every day, but somehow, you are nowhere closer to your goals. As we discussed earlier, one of the reasons why people struggle to succeed is because they haven't yet defined what success means to them. This is what's holding you back—lack of direction. Unfortunately, it manifests in many ways, and another person's definition might not shed some clarity on yours.

The inability to reach your goals can be disheartening, and might even make you stop setting purposeful goals. Your way out of this is to reflect on your steps and find out why things are not working out for you anymore. Below are some common reasons why you might be falling behind:

1. Timeless Ambitions

When will your plan materialise? Deadlines are set for a reason. They keep you motivated and energised to achieve the goals before time lapses. It feels good when you beat deadlines, and you can build on that progress for other tasks. Pursuing goals without a timeline might even create an opportunity for procrastination. As you set targets, make sure you set deadlines for achieving them too.

2. Unquantifiable Objectives

Are your objectives measurable? How do you know that you've achieved them? How can you tell if you came so close, but missed the target by a whisker? If you cannot measure or evaluate your objectives, you need to go back to the drawing board and redefine them.

One of the challenges many young entrepreneurs have today is that they are brimming with brilliant ideas, but lack capital access to fund them. If you are in such a position, one of your goals might be to save some money so you can get your business idea up and running. This sounds like a good goal, but in reality, it is not.

'*Some money*' doesn't tell you anything about how much you need to save. If you set a target of having $10,000 in your savings account by the end of the year, that's more realistic. Every time you check your account balance, you know how far you are from your target, and it motivates you to work even harder. As you get closer to the goal, you are even more charged to hit the target and beat your deadline.

3. Vague Sense of Direction

If your goals lack a sense of direction, you probably won't get anywhere with them. We tend to set goals that are too broad, and then we can't achieve anything. And even if you do, you can't tell whether you succeeded or not. Just like the example above, having 'some money' in your account is such a vague attempt. 'I want to live a healthy life from now on' is another vague target.

What exactly are you planning to do? Do you want to live a healthier life? What must you cut from your current regimen? What changes do you have to make? How can the people living with you support this initiative? *'Starting tomorrow, I will be working out three days a week, and stop eating processed foods'* is more realistic than *'I want to live a healthy life from now on.'*

4. Unrealistic Goals

Grand plans are great. They help you think big and outside the box. A lot of people who think outside the box are successful in their careers. They've built some of the greatest companies and brands we know today. However, you don't want to be the architect of your failure. It's good to set big goals because it challenges you to push your limits. Unfortunately, if you set them too high that you can't attain them, you will suffer burnout, and the disappointment might cripple your success.

5. Irrelevant Targets

You talk about your goals and targets all the time, and honestly, they might sound so good on paper. However, have you ever wondered whether they are relevant? Indeed, there are so many stories of people who achieved success later in their lives, having bummed throughout most of their younger years. However, you can't peg your success on that kind of luck.

Think of your goals in terms of progress. Realizing your goals might be all fun and games, but if their accomplishment adds no value to your life or long term vision, they might be pointless. You will commit a lot of time and resources to your goals, it's only fair that they are relevant to your purpose.

Rules of Personal Success

Big thinking, courage, and determination are some of the features of successful people, and the occasional luck. A lot of these people will tell you, however, that you can only get lucky if you create your luck. Success means conquering everything that stands between you and your goals. The most important of those obstacles is yourself. When people fail, they usually look for reasons why, or people who can take the blame, conveniently absolving themselves of all responsibility. Most of the time, you fail because of self-imposed limitations, conforming to the norm instead of thinking outside the box, and small-mindedness.

Depending on your life's pursuits, the rules of success are not always the same. Set your standards as high as you need them to be, and whatever happens, never apologise for aiming higher. People who are interested in working with you will almost always rise to your expectations. Below are some simple rules that can guide you to success in whatever pursuit your life is about:

1. Self-Assurance

To succeed in life, you must be able to tap into your motivational mindset and evaluate, monitor, and adjust your beliefs, attitudes, and effort. This will help you avoid complacency and keep hitting the high notes that push you closer to reaching your goals. Write down what you want to achieve. Given your targets, define what it means to achieve superior performance. In similar fashion, set guidelines so that you also know how to identify complacent performance. With these benchmarks in place, create an improvement plan to raise your standards whenever you fall short.

2. Solutions in Problems

Have that deep belief that you are heading in the right direction. Trust the process, and be confident in your plans. With this kind of personal power, you should be able to find solutions where most people would see problems. People who approach obstacles with their mindset focused on finding solutions are always creative. Over time, your mind is wired towards finding better ways of getting things done, inspiration, and rewards. By focusing on solutions, you create a culture of adaptation and growth.

3. Time Management

Time is an important resource that everyone has in equal measure, yet some people seem to make more of theirs than others. Time management involves making the most of your present, or what is often referred to as the 'power of now' (Tolle, 2010). Review how you spend your time. Are there any important tasks that you are struggling to move along with? Do you spend more time on other tasks and end up ignoring others? Study your work schedule and identify an order of priorities.

You will be invited to meetings, seminars, and different kinds of events. These are important engagements through which you can build strategic relationships. Show up on time, all the time. This simple rule reminds your hosts of your commitment, and that you recognise their importance and respect them. In any position, there is nothing more powerful than making other people feel significant in your life.

4. Never Lose Perspective

Things will not always go your way. Failure and indifference are normal experiences in life. There are times when your requests will be granted immediately and at other times, you will have to make do with delayed responses. The path to success involves fighting battles— some that might not really be about you—damage control, and fixing problems. These mishaps should never distract you from your objectives.

Don't get caught up in all the drama, because eventually, everything shall pass. If you feel sick, you will get better soon. Someone is throwing a party next door and keeping the entire block awake—the party will end at some point. That ungrateful colleague might not be part of your team for so long. All of these are common experiences that people go through all the time. This is the small stuff. Don't spend your energy worrying about such things. Focus on the end goal.

Ultimately, simplicity will always carry the day. The greatest truth about success is that you can have everything you want, maybe just not at the same time, or on-demand. Use your 24 hours wisely to develop your spirit, work and relationships. Your attention might shift from time to time, your energy levels might not be the same all the time. There are times when you'll need to delegate duties even at home so that you can focus on an important meeting. Sometimes you'll just need to sit down, relax, and unwind with your friends, because it's been such a long time since you were together. Life doesn't need to be complicated. Be mindful, and keep it simple.

Achieving Personal Success

We've discussed how success might not mean the same thing to everyone. Keeping this in mind, we will look at some simple steps that will get you closer to your goals. Note that regardless of the outward recognition and accolades, success will always be a personal thing. Whatever it means to you, success will always begin with having the right attitude. Follow the guidelines below to plan your steps to success:

1. Personal Health

It makes no sense for you to put in all the effort to succeed, yet you forget about the most important piece of the puzzle—you! You are an integral part of the roadmap to success. If you don't take care of yourself, you will suffer burnout, fatigue, and a host of other health concerns that will eventually defeat your purpose. Take care of yourself. Maintain a balanced diet, find time to exercise, and do everything you can to stay energetic.

2. Your Network is Everything

Another important step to success is to build the right networks. Having the right people around you will get you closer to your goals faster, and with better results. Networking is not just about meeting the right people, it is also about exchanging ideas.

No one knows everything, and regardless of your position or job, you are always working for or with people. Be prepared all the time. It is easier to identify new opportunities when you understand what your projects need, and how to sell your vision to like-minded people. Networking is also about impressions. Being impressionable on a subject matter makes you one of the first names people think about when something comes up in your area of expertise.

3. Go the Extra Mile

Don't get comfortable with the ordinary. If everyone is giving 100%, give 101%. We often get excited about quick transformation and results, without realizing that in most cases, this is never sustainable. Small, consistent gains add up to so much. Here's some simple math to explain the exponential value of making a small change in your life for a whole year. Let's say you consistently make just 1% (0.01) effort every day. The exponential value of this change at the end of the year will be as follows:

$$1\% \text{ improvement daily} = 1.01^{365} = 37.78$$

Now, what if you slacked off a bit, in equal measure, every day of the year? The exponential value of this change at the end of the year will be as follows:

$$1\% \text{ regression daily} = 0.99^{365} = 0.03$$

The lesson here is persistence and consistency. Don't worry about the big gains yet. Do something small every day, and keep it up for a year. The results will surprise you..

4. Mentorship

The need for mentorship builds on the knowledge that no one knows everything. To succeed, you must be teachable. Many people have succeeded in your field. Even in personal relationships, many others have experienced challenges similar to those you are going through and made it. Identify the areas of your life you want to improve and focus on how to succeed in life. Find a mentor who has been through something similar and let them guide you on your journey. There's so much you can learn from such an individual that will shed light on your path.

Note, however, that the role of a mentor is not to give you instructions on what to do, but to offer insight, advice, and a different perspective. They might warn you when you are on the wrong path, but eventually, you decide what to do. Another advantage of mentorship is that you might benefit from their networks and connections.

5. Explore New Horizons

Be open-minded and open to new experiences. Very few people have succeeded by shutting everyone out. New experiences give you something different to think about. They challenge you in ways you would never be able to if you didn't think outside the box. Take a break from time to time. Go to new places, talk to new people. This is one of the easiest ways of refreshing your mind and welcoming new ideas.

Even in your relationships, when you are at an impasse, it might be helpful to step outside and go for a walk. Do something different, then come back to the pertinent issue with a different mindset. Taking a step back helps you reflect and see things differently.

6. Practice and Refine

You will learn new skills all the time, and your ability to succeed is directly influenced by how well you can perfect and integrate them into your life. Some people are natural fast learners, others are not. Your speed of learning notwithstanding, spare time to practice new ideas and refine old ones. There is so much technology around you today that you can learn almost anything you want. There are classes on YouTube, and many other reputable learning sites where you can register and enrol in a class. Learn new skills that will improve your life.

The bottom line is that there are many routes to success. Whichever path you follow, define your objectives, then lay out a strategy to achieve it.

Are You There Yet?

After all the effort you have put into your success journey, how do you know whether you have achieved everything you wanted or not? What's the ideal measure of success? Like we mentioned adversely throughout this book, success by definition is different from one person to the next. Here are some simple guidelines that you can use as a yardstick of performance:

1. Adaptability

Success is about growth and change. When you started the journey, you had a target in mind and the only way you could achieve it was by embracing change. All the challenges you have been through, obstacles you overcame, both individually and as a collective unit with your team, culminate into adaptability.

Every challenge forced you to learn new skills and adapt. With each adaptation, you became a more refined member of the society, you learned new ways to take firm control over your life, and eventually came ever closer to your goals. Things probably didn't go well all the time, but you learned how to adapt and keep growing even when all the odds were stacked against you.

2. Knowledge Transfer

There's so much potential in every one of us, most people simply never get to exploit their full range of abilities. If you apply yourself over time, there's so much you can learn and so many skills you can improve. Take your time and reflect on where you were at the beginning and how far you have come. Have you gained any new useful knowledge? Have you learned any new skills? If you have, consider how applying that knowledge has made a difference in your life.

Why is this aspect of self-reflection important? You set yourself apart from everyone else and look at your progress from a different lens. You measure success by what you have achieved so far, instead of comparing yourself with other people, who ran a different race than you did.

Along the way, your professional and personal life

overlapped at some point. Some skills you learned in your professional life made a big difference in your personal life, and vice-versa. Recognise the ripple effect of learning and experience on your skills, adaptability, and pursuit of success. Consider all the lessons you learned and how you implemented them in different places. That is how you measure success.

3. Overall Progress

How much have you accomplished so far? Look back to where you started and everything you have gone through up to this moment. Would you say you have grown in that period? Your thoughts, ideas, everything about you must have experienced some level of transformation. Consider the incremental value of success, based on milestones you accomplish every week, month, and so on as you get closer to your goals.

Success might not be direct, but you certainly can feel the ripple effect of every right step or action towards your end goals. All the actions and steps you take should be making some difference in your life. If this is true, then it all adds up. Despite all the obstacles you've had to overcome, you have made it this far, and that is what progress and success are about.

4. Status in the Community

Another way to measure success is to consider your present status in the community. Every community has people they hold in high regard. These are the people whose voice of reason acts as a guide whenever the community needs one. They are people whose character is beyond refute. What would these people say about you, if they were approached by a stranger and asked to give a vote of confidence in your name? Would they even recognise you?

Your status in the community goes beyond your business activities or anything else you engage in, it speaks to your character. Collaborating with different groups creates an opportunity for more people to get to know you, and learn more about who you are and what you believe in. Success is when such opportunities to collaborate open doors for you to advance and become an even better person with each passing day. In your small way, you make a difference in the community, and the world at large. A positive impact on the people around you will yield natural success.

5. Your Passions and Desires

What are you passionate about? Do you even like what you do? Are you comfortable with life as it is? Success is being at that point where you love and enjoy doing what you do. It goes beyond your earnings or job title. It is that sense of gratitude and satisfaction knowing that you made a difference in someone's life.

Many people never get to enjoy this opportunity—to do something they love, and enjoy the process while at it. Circumstances generally dictate people's lives, and only a handful ever find themselves in this kind of privilege. Doing the things you love heightens your personal development through the activities and habits you learn each day. It eventually improves the quality of your life by achieving different goals, which were otherwise unrelated.

CHAPTER
SEVEN

The Psychology of Creativity and Productivity

Productivity and creativity are two aspects of success that usually coexist, but in many cases, might also exist in perpetual tension. These two might share some similarities and value in your pursuit of success, but don't be confused, they are dissimilar. For a start, while you can measure productivity, it's difficult to apply the same metrics to creativity.

Productivity involves efficient and effective planning and scheduling throughout your busy day. Creativity, on the other hand, generally demands letting go of all the inhibitions that come with structure and the systematic methods of going about your day. Creativity thrives on freedom, while productivity thrives on structure, and in many cases, rigidity.

The concept of creativity generally derives its purpose from knowledge. It is about applying your skills and knowledge in a different way to come up with something unique. We talk of thinking outside the box so casually, but to do that, you must first gain knowledge of whatever exists outside the box, or risk getting lost in oblivion.

The creative process shuns irrelevant knowledge. There are critical moments in life where your creative mind is called into action. You can only thrive in such instances when you are knowledgeable about the subject matter.

There's so much innovation in the world today, and with that, many organizations and even people find themselves obsolete for lack of innovation. Creativity and knowledge are prerequisites for innovation. Some more skills and activities are connected to this process which you might not always be able to measure.

Even with everything we know about creativity, many people still believe that working long hours is more productive than taking a break, or a day off work. The qualities that we consider as a definition of a successful day at work are pretty much a list of items you'd have in your to-do list. Yet, more freedom in planning your day and time might yield better results. The big question is, therefore, in your honest opinion, when do you feel you have proven your worth: when you are creative or productive?

Creativity can be confusing at times. The process, for many people, is usually prolonged and messy. The inspiration for brilliant ideas comes in the weirdest and most absurd moments. Rarely do the light bulb moments come to you sitting at your desk, staring into your computer. The ideas come to you on your morning run, when you're taking a bath, or even when you encounter a random stranger on the street. These ideas barely come to you at the urgency you desire. Going by this process alone, creativity almost feels like the exact opposite of what we expect productivity to be about.

Unfortunately, most workspaces today are built for productivity, with little regard for creativity. Some people even joke about productivity as the place where creativity comes to die. Like success, you have to redefine your idea of productivity in light of your creative processes, because just getting things done will not cut it.

Two Birds, One Stone?

Going by our discussion above, the pertinent question in your mind right now is whether you can achieve both productivity and creativity simultaneously. Take note, that the implied idea of creativity involves carefree individuals, artsy people whose success transcends rules, time limits, and at times, the law. Productivity, on the other hand, is underpinned by a near-obsession with maximum efficiency and results.

From time to time, the elements of productivity and creativity might appear as different as heaven and earth, raising even more doubts than certainty of whether you can tap into both to realise your goals. Bringing them into perspective, you must have both to succeed. One can never exist without the other.

It is through the creative process that your visions come to life. Creativity is about disrupting the status quo, challenging the system, rethinking and reshaping the way you work and live. Productivity is the grit, process, and determination that goes into turning an idea from concept to reality, and in most cases, under uncomfortable situations. Circumstances are not always ideal for productivity, but the end result is sustainability.

In the section below, we will discuss different approaches you can use to tap into both your productive and creative juices to build the successful life you deserve.

1. Admit Mistakes

Don't ever be afraid to make mistakes. Accept your responsibility when things don't work out, and move past it. One of the reasons why people waste a lot of time in their creative processes is because they are too afraid to admit they made a mistake. It gets worse when you've spent a lot of time and resources to create that mistake. It doesn't matter how much you've invested in a mistake; if it's not right, it never will be.

Be bold and change the direction. Recognise that a mistake happened, and you've hit a dead-end, or you're close to one. You don't have to stick it to the end for a dead idea for the sake of productivity. As soon as you realise that an idea is not working, abandon it and move on to something else. In the long run, cutting your losses will prove to be more productive, and even give you the motivation to avoid similar mistakes on your next idea.

2. Collector's Inspiration

Reading is the perfect sweet spot where productivity and creativity collide. Note down the things that inspire you while reading, either save them as bookmarks or print them for future reference. Apart from reading, you can also collect inspirational items like artefacts, pictures, and postcards. This collection can become your first-aid inspiration kit whenever you need something to spark your creative juices.

3. Ditch the Routine

A new environment or experience might be good for your creativity. When you need some inspiration from time to time, break away from your routine. This can help you see things differently, change your thought process, and you might even chance upon an external trigger that gives you the spark you need to get your creativity going.

Before you ditch your routine, make sure your disruption is not haphazard. Go at it with a purpose, otherwise, you might lose yourself in the process. A break might do you some good, but if unchecked, it can also expose you to unnecessary distractions that are not good for your productivity or creativity, and in the long run, might interfere with your mindset.

4. Follow Your Passion

Creativity and passion go hand in hand. If you are not passionate about something, you might put in lacklustre efforts from time to time, and probably never bring out the full creative element. You can cultivate your passion by learning as much as you can about the subject. Learn from experts in the field, find out about the latest news and advancements in technology around that sector. Find out what customers are looking for, what trends they think are outdated, and so on.

If you are not passionate about something, the most you might do is shallow research on Google to learn the basics. You can also cultivate your passion by pursuing a purpose through it. This is similar to being on a mission, challenged by everything around you, and the desire to complete the mission and see what's on the other side.

5. Identify Opportunities Around You

You never know where or when you'll find your next creative idea. Creativity has no limit, and an idea can come to you when you least expect it. Your productive session at work might have ended with your shift, but that doesn't stop you from being creative. You can find inspiration everywhere around you. It might be a conversation you overheard on your way home or an ad that flashed across your smartphone.

With all the ideas that come to mind, the secret is how to connect them—especially those ideas that seem unrelated at first—and find inspiration in the most unlikely places. This is also proof that your creative exploits are not limited to your productive time at work. Thus, you can achieve both.

6. Standing Out

The perfect recipe for productivity and creativity usually depends on the nature of your profession or business. Whether it is an in-person business or one that thrives on scale operations, find a way to stand out from everyone else. You cannot differentiate and prove to your customers or clients that yours is a unique offering without creativity. Even with creativity, productivity comes in through the effort you make to sell the unique idea to a customer.

Improve Your Productivity

We all have 24 hours in a day. The difference comes in how you use yours. Given this finite amount of time, you can improve productivity either by working smarter around the time you have or putting in more hours. Unfortunately, most people who put in more hours under the guise of being productive never really do. Productivity is not about how long you work on something, but how much more you can do with the little time you have. Below are some strategies that can help you improve your productivity:

1. Track Your Time

Do you know how much time you commit to and spend on tasks? Are you spending more on some tasks than others? We usually assume that we can perform some mental math and allocate time accordingly to all tasks, but that is never the case. Why don't you proactively track your time? How much time are you spending on social media, checking emails, working, or idly roaming around the office? The results might shock you.

2. Reasonable Breaks

Breaks might sound like taking time off your productive schedule, but scheduling them properly can help you break the monotony and concentrate better. Regular breaks are helpful, especially when you are working on a huge task. You come back from the break rejuvenated, and agile enough to maintain a good level of performance. Working on a big task without breaks is almost always counterproductive.

3. Create Mini Deadlines

Away from your official deadlines, challenge yourself with smaller, self-imposed deadlines. This gives you a push to focus and handle your deliverables much faster. Creating such deadlines is usually productive, especially when you are working on an open-ended assignment. Create a deadline and honour it.

4. Avoid Meetings

This might come as a surprise, but meetings are some of the biggest time wasters you'll ever come across. How many times have you attended a meeting, only to wonder why the agenda couldn't have been summed up in a three-sentence email? A lot of meetings are quite unproductive, yet we still schedule and attend them, and inevitably complain about them too. Before you schedule the next meeting, think about the agenda and ask yourself whether you can achieve the same goals through a phone call or an email.

If you have to attend a meeting, try to set a time limit, and if possible, hold standing meetings. There is less comfort in such meetings, and people generally move their points along faster so that they can get on with other things.

5. The Multitasking Demon

Multitasking is quite the paradox. Those who do it assume that they are very productive, while the entire premise of multitasking points to someone unable to manage their time accordingly. Multitaskers often assume that this is an incredible skill that increases their efficiency. Unfortunately, the reverse is true. You lose more time trying to complete several tasks at the same time, than if you focused on one task at a time. Create a habit of committing to one task, getting it across the line, and moving on to the next one.

If you want to put in more productivity in your work, don't fall for the temptation to work longer hours, or add more work to your packed calendar. Calmly review your schedule, and instead of working harder, look for ways you can work smarter.

Improve Your Creativity

Did you know that in the near future, scientists might be able to boost creativity by zapping the brain? This is an interesting approach that monitors brain activity and the flow of blood in the frontopolar cortex (Lucchiari et al., 2018). You've probably seen a lot of this in the movies, and would probably want to leave it at that, right? I mean, imagine having to get your brain stimulated whenever you need some creativity. How often would you have to do that? Would it be safe? What would be the limit? How long before you zap your brain to toast?

You don't have to get there though. Think of creativity like your muscles; you have to exercise from time to time to stay fit and go beyond the comfort zone. There are many instances where you need to be creative every other day, and honestly, zapping your brain every other day will probably send you to an early grave—we don't want that! The good news is that you can improve your creativity without going through such measures. Here are some simple tips to get you there:

1. Regular Exercise

What if you could just try? Seriously though, have you even tried to think of something creative, or a creative way to do something? There is no magic or fairy tale behind creativity. It is putting one foot in front of the other, and with whatever knowledge you might have, you'll come up with something amazing.

You use the same skills you'd use to accomplish every other task for creativity. The only difference is that instead of following the same routine process, you switch things up a bit. What most people don't realise is that when you try to be creative in your actions, thoughts, or behaviour, you almost always succeed. It's so simple—your brain gets better at something the more you keep doing it.

2. Change Your Environment

When it comes to improving creativity, at times all you need is a change of environment, even in the slightest sense possible. Changing your environment doesn't necessarily mean going to a different room or place, but if that works for you, then go ahead. Subtle changes like opening the curtains, a hot cup of coffee, changing the setup or orientation of your desk, or adjusting your seat slightly, can do the trick.

You might not always have complete control over your environment, but if you can change anything in there, go ahead. Talking to the same old people every other day, or looking at the same things on your walls and desk all the time, might not be good for your creativity.

3. Challenge Yourself

Challenges catalyse your brain to think better and come up with ideal solutions. If you come home but your key cannot open the door, your brain immediately starts looking for solutions. You bang on the door or ring the bell, hoping that if someone is inside, they can come open it for you. If no one is inside, you will try jiggling the key a bit and give it another try. You might even get a bobby pin and try some MacGyver stuff on the locks.

4. Collaborate

An unpredictable flash of genius might spur innovation from time to time, but if you want to make it sustainable, you have to create a system that supports that creative spark. This is possible when you work with other people. If you are uncertain about something, go out and learn. Read, talk to experts in the field, and so on. Working with different people gives you the benefit of tapping into their perspective. A new line of thought can give you the ultimate creative boost you need.

CONCLUSION

People often talk about having their day planned out, yet only a handful follow these plans accordingly. So many people lose the plot as soon as they step out of the house, and never finish everything on that list. Others don't accomplish anything at all. What's even more fascinating is that amidst all the chaos and confusion that consumes a majority of the population, some people defy the odds and complete everything on their to-do list, not once or twice, but every day.

If you've been in such a position where you can barely get through everything on your list, what's your reason? There's so much on your mind? You got a lot of things going on? Maybe you are such a spontaneous person, you don't need all the rules and rigidity? All these are excuses to conceal the fact that you lack self-discipline.

We've discussed self-discipline at length, highlighting many ways it manifests, the challenges posed, and how you can take back control and be in charge of your life. The thing about self-discipline is that it is a personal choice. You can learn from people, you can follow their examples, but eventually, it comes down to you. What is your life about? What are you working towards? How far are you from your goals? ...And that's if you have any goals in the first place. Who do you want to be in five or ten years?

When was the last time you had an honest conversation with yourself and audited your life? Yes, auditing isn't limited to the financial sector or tech systems audit. People say a lot of things about you, some that soothe your ego, and others that are outright untrue. The problem is, most of these people don't know you as well as you do yourself. They know the version of you that you present before them. They know the person you want them to think you are. But deep down, you know the truth. If you are struggling with self-discipline, you know it, and you know how much it has cost you so far. The question is, will you keep losing, or are you ready to turn things around and be the champion you are supposed to be?

One important lesson that resonates throughout this book is to be real. Embrace your reality and work with it. Many people live in denial, and it only pulls you back. If things are not working out, however many times you try to convince yourself that they are, they will not. First, second, third...umpteenth opportunities have passed you by. None of this is by chance or bad luck. You create your luck, and without self-discipline, all your effort is futile.

People talk about productivity in terms of

personalities or the kind of work that they are assigned. Here's a shocker—none of that matters. Productivity is about how disciplined you are. People procrastinate all the time, regardless of their personality or the kind of task they are assigned. It takes a lot of discipline to stay on track and focus on your deliverables. This is how you ensure that at the end of the day, your to-do list is not a cemetery where less important tasks find their eternal resting place. Everything that makes it onto your to-do list is there for a reason, so keep your head down, and do the work. You don't need supervision or a reminder. Do the work because it matters, and never lose sight of your goals. This is discipline.

If you need to see some improvement in any aspect of your life, real growth, development, and maturity, you must practice self-discipline. It is about creating positive habits and making them a routine. Something as simple as waking up on time and making your bed will go a long way if you keep it up every other day. Self-discipline is at the centre of the lives of successful personalities you know today.

Here's the thing, behind all the tough talk, self-discipline is not that difficult, so don't fret. It is simply about commitment. Start small; start from wherever you are. Start with a list of three or five things you must accomplish each day, then keep it up for a week, a month, and so on. Get things done, and whatever happens, don't stop.

Self-discipline is like a muscle. Simple routine exercises make it stronger and nourish it to serve you better. The best thing about it is that as you become more familiar with it, you realise wholesome benefits in every aspect of your life. There will be temptations along the way, but don't lose sight of your goals. If you fall, get up, dust yourself off, and keep going. Remember that the less you feel like doing something, yet you beat the temptation and do it, the stronger your self-discipline gets.

The purpose of this book is to nudge you to go out of your comfort zone and pursue the life you want. Be more organised, find true happiness, pursue success, and achieve great things. You have so much to live for, why let it all go to waste?

Here's something to ponder:

Are you busy, or are you busy trying to look busy?

References

Barboza, G. (2017). I Will Pay Tomorrow, or Maybe the Day After. Credit Card Repayment, Present Biased and Procrastination. Economic Notes, 47(2-3), 455–494. https://doi.org/10.1111/ecno.12106

Brooks, R. B., & Goldstein, S. (2003). The power of resilience : Achieving balance, confidence, and personal strength in your life. Contemporary Books.

Dr. Daniel Fox. (2018). How You Can Control Your Emotions with Dr. Fox - Affective Regulation. In YouTube. https://www.youtube.com/watch?v=nrqfSvNIuS0

Fagan, D. (2020, January 29). Real-Life Examples of Opportunity Cost. Open Vault Blog; Federal Reserve Bank of St. Louis. https://www.stlouisfed.org/open-vault/2020/january/real-life-examples-opportunity-cost

Franck, H., & Krohn, M. (2018). Improving Lives: Self-discipline, Disciplining the Self and Self-less Discipline. Academy of Management Proceedings, 2018(1), 13956. https://doi.org/10.5465/ambpp.2018.13956symposium

References

Georgetown University. (2016, April 14). Electrical
    Brain Stimulation Enhances Creativity,
    Researchers Say. Georgetown University.
    https://www.georgetown.edu/news/electrical-
    brain-stimulation-enhances-creativity-
    researchers-say/

Hurriyati, E. A., Fitriana, E., Cahyadi, S., & Srisayekti,
    W. (2020). Control and Emotional Reactivity
    Levels: Which One, Positive or Negative
    Emotional Reactivity Links with Effortful
    Control? Humaniora, 11(1), 35.
    https://doi.org/10.21512/humaniora.v11i1.618
    8

Kohnen, J. (2009). Executive Focus: Your Life and
    Career. Quality Management Journal, 16(2), 61–
    61.
    https://doi.org/10.1080/10686967.2009.11918
    229

Labier, D. (2016). Modern madness : The hidden link
    between work and emotional conflict. Open
    Road Media.

Lucchiari, C., Sala, P. M., & Vanutelli, M. E. (2018).
    Promoting Creativity Through Transcranial
    Direct Current Stimulation (tDCS). A Critical
    Review. Frontiers in Behavioral Neuroscience,
    12. https://doi.org/10.3389/fnbeh.2018.00167

Lyon, A. (2018). What is Self-Actualization? In
    YouTube.
    https://www.youtube.com/watch?v=VfHw60
    YGS_E

Maslow, A. H., Stephens, D. C., & Heil, G. (1998).
    Maslow on Management. John Wiley.

O'neill, J., Conzemius, A., & Commodore, C. (2006).
    The Power of SMART goals: Using goals to
    improve student learning. Solution Tree.

Özaslan, G. (2018). The Essential Meaning of Self-Actualization via Principalship: A Phenomenological Study. Journal of Qualitative Research in Education, 6(2), 1–16. https://doi.org/10.14689/issn.2148-2624.1.6c2s1m

Reuben, E., Sapienza, P., & Zingales, L. (2008). Procrastination and Impatience. Centre For Economic Policy Research.

TED. (2016). Inside the mind of a master procrastinator | Tim Urban. In YouTube. https://www.youtube.com/watch?v=arj7oStG LkU

TED. (2019). How to build your confidence -- and spark it in others | Brittany Packnett. In YouTube. https://www.youtube.com/watch?v=b5ZESp OAolU

Teo, A. C. (2012). Why procrastinate? : A teenagers' guide to overcoming procrastination. Armour Pub.

Tolle, E. (2010). The Power of Now: A Guide to Spiritual Enlightenment. In Google Books. New World Library. https://books.google.co.ke/books?id=sQYqR CIhFAMC&printsec=frontcover&dq=the+po wer+of+now&hl=en&sa=X&ved=2ahUKEwi V6enAt_XvAhU8CGMBHXRHAyEQ6AEwA HoECAIQAg#v=onepage&q=the%20power %20of%20now&f=false

Vee, G. (2015). How do you stay focused on your goals? In YouTube. https://www.youtube.com/watch?v=ylfxDMv RyLs